Collins

GCSE Revision

Physical Education

Physical Education

GCSE

Revision Guide

Matthew Fleet

Contents

Contents

The Structure and Functions of the Musculo-skeletal System 1

You must be able to:

- Explain the structure and functions of the musculo-skeletal system
- Apply the functions of the skeleton to physical activity and sport.

The Functions of the Skeleton

The protection of vital organs

- **Bones** are extremely strong.
- One of their main functions is to protect the organs, for example the ribs protect the heart and lungs.

Muscle attachment

- Muscles are attached to bones at each end by a thick tendon.
- When the muscles contract, they exert a force on the bones.

Cartilage

- Cartilage is a firm tissue that is softer than bone.
- It acts as a shock absorber between bones.

Joints for movement

There are three different types of joint.

- Fixed joints have no space between the bones, therefore no movement is possible, for example the skull.
- Slightly moveable joints are separated by cartilage and allow small amounts of movement, for example the vertebral column.
- Freely moveable joints contain a membrane that surrounds the joint; this membrane contains synovial fluid, e.g. the knee.

Platelets

- The bones produce **platelets**, which help blood to clot when the skin is damaged.
- They are tiny cells with no nucleus.

Red and white blood cell production

- Bones are responsible for red and white blood cell production.
- Red and white blood cells destroy viruses and bacteria, and are produced in the bone marrow of major bones.
- **Red blood cells** carry oxygen all over the body in red haemoglobin to where it is needed. Red blood cells only have space for haemoglobin and do not have a nucleus.
- **White blood cell** production is vital for protecting against disease and infection. White blood cells have a nucleus.

Storage of calcium and phosphorus

- Bones store vital minerals such as calcium and phosphorus. These minerals make bones and teeth strong.

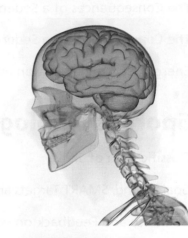

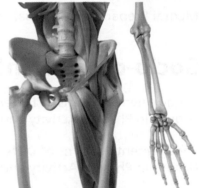

Blood

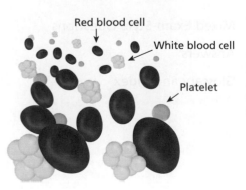

Red blood cell

White blood cell

Platelet

The Classification of Bones

Long bones:
* are longer than they are wide
* have a soft centre surrounded by a hard outer casing
* are used as levers to enable the body to move
* examples include the fibula and tibia, the long leg bones that are used in cycling, running and swimming.

Short bones:
* are approximately as long as they are wide
* have large quantities of bone marrow to make blood vessels
* examples include the carpals and tarsals in the wrists and feet
* are weight-bearing bones
* are often shock-absorbing bones.

Flat bones:
* are flat and particularly strong
* have muscles attached that provide protection
* examples include the scapula (shoulder) and the cranium (skull).

Irregular bones:
* all remaining bones are classed as irregular bones
* are often unusual in appearance
* uses include both protection and muscle attachment
* examples include the bones that make up the vertebral column (spine) and mandible (jaw).

> **Key Point**
>
> A joint is where two or more bones meet.

Bones of the Skeleton

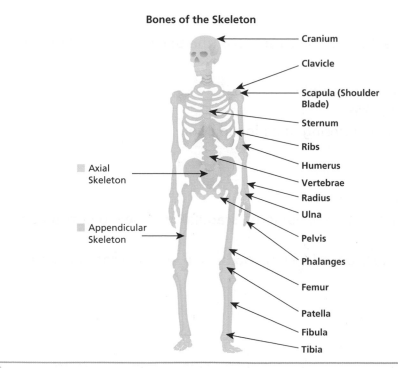

Cranium
Clavicle
Scapula (Shoulder Blade)
Sternum
Ribs
Humerus
Vertebrae
Radius
Ulna
Pelvis
Phalanges
Femur
Patella
Fibula
Tibia

Axial Skeleton
Appendicular Skeleton

> **Key Points**
>
> * Bones are the pieces of white hard tissue that make up the skeletal system.
> * The skeleton is the body's internal framework of bones; it is made up of 206 bones and peak bone density is usually at the age of 30.

Quick Test

1. Name the functions of the skeleton.
2. Name the three different types of joint.
3. Name the four classifications of bones.

> **Key Words**
>
> **Bones**
> **Platelets**
> **Red blood cells**
> **White blood cells**

The Structure and Functions of the Musculo-skeletal System 2

You must be able to:

- Explain the structure and functions of the joints
- Apply the functions of joints to physical activity and sport
- Identify movement possibilities at the joints.

The Classification of Joints

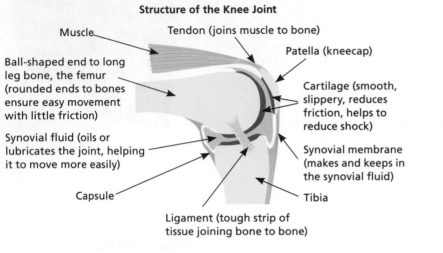

Structure of the Knee Joint

Muscle

Tendon (joins muscle to bone)

Patella (kneecap)

Ball-shaped end to long leg bone, the femur (rounded ends to bones ensure easy movement with little friction)

Cartilage (smooth, slippery, reduces friction, helps to reduce shock)

Synovial fluid (oils or lubricates the joint, helping it to move more easily)

Synovial membrane (makes and keeps in the synovial fluid)

Capsule

Tibia

Ligament (tough strip of tissue joining bone to bone)

> **Key Point**
>
> Nearly all joints are **synovial joints**, which are moveable and contain a lubricating liquid called synovial fluid. They are usually located in your limbs where movement is required.

Pivot:
- one bone rotates around another
- an example is the neck, which rotates around the atlas and axis (the bones of the vertebrae).

Hinge:
- flexion and extension is the only movement possible
- examples include the elbow, knee and ankle
- the movement is similar to the opening and closing of a hinged door.

Ball and socket:
- allow most movement of all the joints
- allow arms and legs to move in almost any direction
- examples include the shoulder (articulating bones: humerus, scapula) and the hip (articulating bones: pelvis, femur)
- **movement patterns** include flexion, extension, adduction, abduction, internal rotation and external rotation.

Condyloid:
- allows circular movement
- examples include the wrist
- movement patterns include flexion, extension, abduction, adduction and circumduction.

Articulating:
- these are the bones that move during activity
- examples include the knee (articulating bones: femur, tibia) and the elbow (articulating bones: humerus, radius and ulna).

Movement Possibilities at Joints

Movement patterns	Description	Example
Flexion	Decreasing the angle at a joint	-Running and jumping movements at the hip and knee -Throwing and racket sports action at the elbow
Extension	Increasing the angle at a joint	-Running and jumping movements at the hip and knee -Throwing and racket sports action at the elbow
Horizontal Flexion	Moving arm forwards in horizontal plane (starting from abducted position)	Throwing and racket sports movement at the shoulder
Horizontal Extension	Returning arm to the abducted position (starting from abducted position)	Throwing and racket sports movement at the shoulder
Hyper Flexion	Flexion of a limb beyond the normal limit	Running and jumping movements at the hip and knee
Hyper Extension	The excessive joint movement in which the angle is straightened beyond its normal range	Running and jumping movements at the hip and knee
Adduction	Moving towards the midline of the body	Adduction of the shoulder, in backstroke
Abduction	Moving away from the midline of the body	Taking one leg away from the other, like in side stepping
Rotation	Moving a limb in a circular motion in either direction	Movement in racket sports
Circumduction	Combination of flexion, extension, abduction and adduction	The shoulder, hip, wrist and ankle are all examples of joints that can undertake circumduction
Pronation	The forearm, pronation is the movement of turning the palm over to face downwards	Wrist action in racket sports
Supination	Is the opposite movement of pronation, turning the palm up or forwards	Wrist action in racket sports
Plantar-Flexion	Extension of the ankle, pointing of the foot and toes	-Running, kicking and jumping movement at the ankle
Dorsiflexion	Flexion of the foot in an upward direction	-Running, kicking and jumping movement at the ankle

Quick Test

1. Name the classifications of joints.
2. Describe the movement pattern of flexion.
3. Describe the movement pattern of abduction.

Key Words

Movement patterns

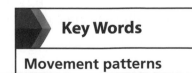

The Structure and Functions of the Musculo-skeletal System 3

You must be able to:

- Identify the role of ligaments and tendons
- Explain the classification of muscle types.

The Role of Ligaments and Tendons

Ligaments:

- connect bones to bones
- are very strong
- an example would be the cruciate knee ligaments.

Tendons:

- connect muscles to bones
- an example would be the Achilles tendon.

Classification and Characteristics of Muscle Types

- There are four different types of muscle (cardiac, voluntary, involuntary and fixator).
- Muscles are made up of tiny string-like fibres.
- Muscles contract by shortening.
- Nerve messages sent from the brain cause muscle contraction.

Voluntary muscles:

- are attached to the end of bones
- are controlled by yourself, through conscious thought
- for example, choosing to move your arms up to catch a ball.

Involuntary muscles:

- are located around organs
- are located in the blood vessels
- move without conscious thought.

Cardiac muscle:

- is only found in your heart
- it never gets tired
- it moves without conscious control
- it is used to help pump blood around the body.

Fixator muscles:

- are muscles that help to stabilise a joint
- for example, the rotator cuff stabilises the bicep.

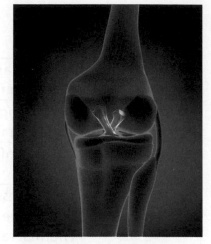

Cruciate knee ligaments

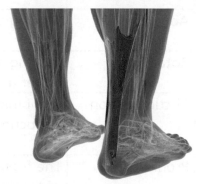

Achilles tendon

Cardiac muscle

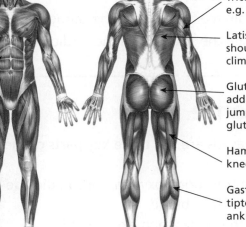

Deltoids create abduction at the shoulder and raise your arm sideways, e.g. swimming arm action.

Pectorals create adduction at the shoulder across the chest, e.g. press-ups.

Biceps cause flexion at the elbow, e.g. chin-ups.

Abdominals allow you to flex your trunk, e.g. sit-ups.

Quadriceps make extension of the leg possible at the knee, e.g. squats, kicking.

Trapezius allows rotation of the shoulders, e.g. cricket bowling action.

Triceps create extension at the elbow, e.g. press-ups, throwing.

Latissimus allows adduction at the shoulder behind your back, e.g. rope climb.

Gluteals allow extension, abduction and adduction at the hip, e.g. squats, jumping. (Gluteus Maximus is the biggest gluteal.)

Hamstrings allow flexion of the leg at the knee, e.g. sprinting (leg action recovery).

Gastrocnemius allows you to stand on tiptoes, by creating extension at the ankle, e.g. sprinting (start).

Antagonistic Pairs of Muscles

Pairs of muscles create movement.

Agonist:
- the muscle shortens
- the muscle is the prime mover
- for example in a bicep curl, the biceps brachii is the agonist.

Antagonist:
- the muscle lengthens
- the muscle relaxes
- for example in a bicep curl, the triceps brachii is the antagonist.

Characteristics of fast and slow twitch muscle fibre types

Characteristics	Type I (slow twitch)	Type IIa (fast twitch)	Type IIx (sometimes called type IIb, fast twitch)
Oxygen use	Use oxygen	Use oxygen	Do not use oxygen
Colour	Red	Red	White
Contraction Speed and Strength	Slow	Fast	Very fast and powerful
Levels of Fatigue	Do not get tired easily	Partially resistant to fatigue	Very high
Sporting Example	Marathon runner	400-metre runner	100-metre sprinter

> **Key Point**
>
> It is important to remember that muscles usually only pull and when they contract they shorten in length. For example, when straightening your leg, the quadriceps are the agonist and hamstrings are antagonist.

> **Quick Test**
>
> 1. Explain the role of ligaments.
> 2. Explain the role of tendons.
> 3. What are the agonist and antagonist?
> 4. What are the three different muscle fibre types?

> **Key Words**
>
> Voluntary muscles
> Involuntary muscles
> Cardiac muscle
> Fixator muscles

The Structure and Functions of the Cardio-respiratory System 1

You must be able to:

- Explain the functions of the cardio-vascular system
- Explain the structure of the cardio-vascular system.

Physical Performance

The heart, blood and blood vessels are the three key parts of the cardio-vascular system.

- The cardio-vascular system transports oxygen, carbon dioxide and nutrients around the body in blood.
- The system is able to cool the body when exercising by transporting blood closer to the skin.
- The system has a double circuit, with blood entering into the heart twice, through each side once.
- Deoxygenated blood is carried back to the heart.
- Oxygenated blood is carried away from the heart.

Structure of the Cardio-vascular System and Route

Cardiac cycle

1. **Atrial systole**: atria contract and force blood into the ventricles.
2. **Ventricular systole**: ventricles contract and force the blood into the arteries.
3. At the same time the atria and ventricles relax and blood begins to flow back into them from the veins.
4. **Diastole**: muscles of both atria and ventricles relax.
5. The heart fills with blood and the cycle repeats.

Pathway of blood through the heart

Deoxygenated blood passes through these blood vessels, valves and parts of the heart.

1. Vena cava → 2. Right atrium → 3. Tricuspid → 4. Right ventricle → 5. Semilunar → 6. Pulmonary artery → 7. Lungs

Oxygenated blood passes through these blood vessels, valves and parts of the heart.

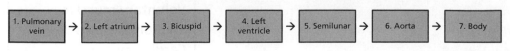

1. Pulmonary vein → 2. Left atrium → 3. Bicuspid → 4. Left ventricle → 5. Semilunar → 6. Aorta → 7. Body

Key Points

- Deoxygenated blood does not contain oxygen; it has been used by the muscles and is on its way back to the heart.

- Oxygenated blood is carried away from the heart to the muscles or organs that require it.

- Circulatory system – transports essential bodily substances around the body. It is a double circuit made up of heart and blood vessels.

Structure and Function of Arteries, Capillaries and Veins

- **Arteries** – carry oxygenated blood away from the heart. They are the largest of the vessels.
- **Capillaries** – are the smallest vessels and they form a network all over the body, which connects veins and arteries.
- **Veins** – carry deoxygenated blood towards the heart.

The mechanisms required

- **Vasoconstriction** – blood vessels constrict, getting smaller and tighter, reducing blood flow.
- **Vasodilation** – blood vessels widen and allow increased blood flow.
- **Vascular shunt** – when exercising and blood needs to be redistributed around the body with more oxygen going to the working muscles.

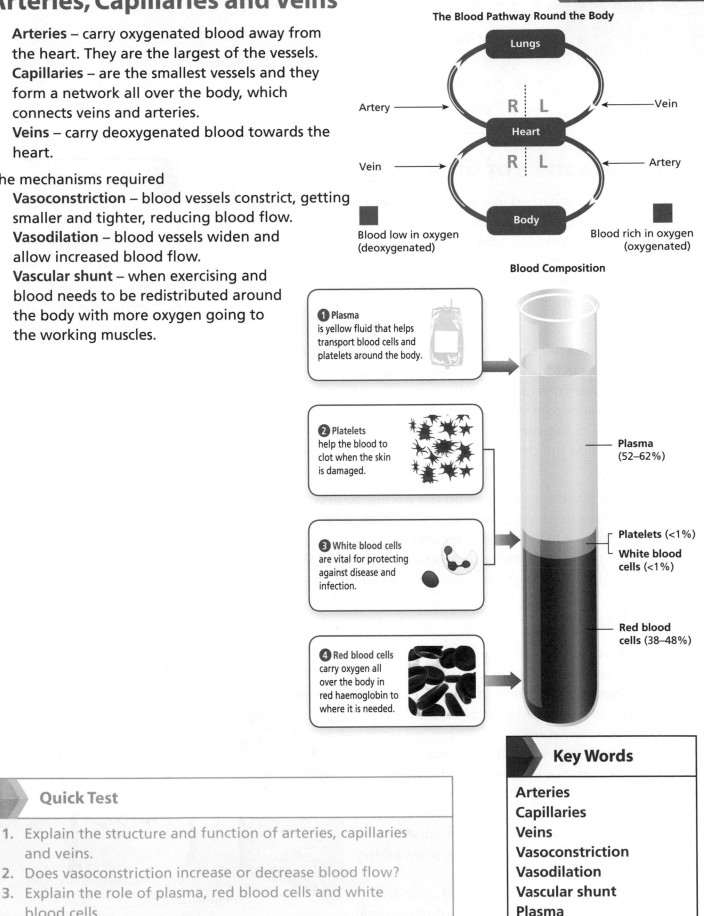

The Blood Pathway Round the Body

Lungs

Artery ⟶ R | L ⟵ Vein

Heart

Vein ⟶ R | L ⟵ Artery

Body

Blood low in oxygen (deoxygenated)

Blood rich in oxygen (oxygenated)

Blood Composition

1 Plasma is yellow fluid that helps transport blood cells and platelets around the body.

2 Platelets help the blood to clot when the skin is damaged.

3 White blood cells are vital for protecting against disease and infection.

4 Red blood cells carry oxygen all over the body in red haemoglobin to where it is needed.

Plasma (52–62%)

Platelets (<1%)
White blood cells (<1%)

Red blood cells (38–48%)

Quick Test

1. Explain the structure and function of arteries, capillaries and veins.
2. Does vasoconstriction increase or decrease blood flow?
3. Explain the role of plasma, red blood cells and white blood cells.

Key Words

Arteries
Capillaries
Veins
Vasoconstriction
Vasodilation
Vascular shunt
Plasma

The Structure and Functions of the Cardio-respiratory System 2

You must be able to:

- Explain the structure and function of the respiratory system
- Explain the mechanics of breathing
- Explain aerobic and anaerobic respiration.

The Mechanics of Breathing

- The air that is breathed in is filtered and warmed as it passes in through the nose and mouth.
- It then travels down the trachea and into bronchioles in the lungs.
- It then passes into the alveoli, which are tiny air sacs.
- Gases are then exchanged, with oxygen passing into the blood and carbon dioxide being removed.

Inspiration

1. Intercostal muscles contract, inflating the ribcage (during exercise the pectorals and sternocleidomastoid are used to create greater force and speed).
2. The diaphragm contracts, pulling downward to increase the volume of the chest.
3. Pressure inside the chest is decreased and air is sucked in.

Expiration

4. Intercostal muscles relax, causing the ribcage to drop inwards and downwards (during exercise the **abdominal muscles** are used to remove carbon dioxide quicker).
5. Diaphragm relaxes, moving back upwards, reducing the volume.
6. Pressure inside the chest rises and air is forced out.

Lung Volumes

- **Vital capacity** is the maximum amount of air that can be breathed in or out.
- Vital capacity is measured using a spirometer.
- **Tidal volume** is the amount of air that enters the lungs when at rest.
- For an adult the average tidal volume is 500 ml.
- **Expiratory reserve volume** is the highest amount of air that can be breathed out (above tidal volume) during forceful exhalation.
- **Inspiratory reserve volume** is the additional air breathed in (above tidal volume) when taking a deep breath.
- **Residual volume** is the amount of air in the lungs that cannot be breathed out of maximal exhalation.

Key Point

During exercise:

- breathing gets quicker and deeper
- heart rate and circulation increase
- vasodilation prevents blood pressure getting too high
- vascular shunt mechanism directs the blood to the working muscles
- blood vessels vasodilate (widen), or vasoconstrict (constrict)
- sweat is produced and cools the body.

The Capillary Network Around the Alveoli

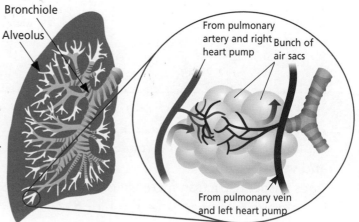

Bronchiole

Alveolus

From pulmonary artery and right heart pump

Bunch of air sacs

From pulmonary vein and left heart pump

- To develop **anaerobic capacity**, working at high intensity for short periods of time, for example, fartlek training or interval training, is most effective.

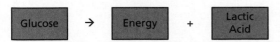

Glucose → Energy + Lactic Acid

Excess post-exercise oxygen consumption (EPOC)

- **EPOC** is the rise in consumption of oxygen after excessive exercise.
- It is where the body is trying to replace the oxygen debt after vigorous exercise, when a participant is trying to recover.
- When we have exhausted oxygen supplies, lactic acid is produced as a harmful by-product.
- Breathing rate is increased to recover the oxygen debt, with shallow breaths.

High altitude training as a form of aerobic training

- Less oxygen in the air and oxygen-carrying capacity is reduced.
- The body compensates by making more red blood cells.
- Can be beneficial to endurance athletes.
- Adversely, it can be difficult to complete training.
- Altitude sickness can affect performance/training.
- The benefits are short term.

Energy Sources

Fat:
- provides a concentrated source of energy
- gives fuel for low- to moderate-intensity aerobic activity.

Protein:
- builds and repairs muscles
- should make up 15% of an individual's diet.

Carbohydrate:
- a highly efficient energy source as it requires less oxygen
- the main fuel for your muscles
- vital during high-intensity exercise when enough oxygen cannot be processed
- fuels aerobic and anaerobic activity.

> **Key Point**
>
> Energy is the capacity to do work; it allows you to sustain physical or mental performance.

> **Quick Test**
>
> 1. What is the difference between aerobic and anaerobic respiration?
> 2. What type of activity does fat provide energy for?
> 3. What type of activity do carbohydrates provide energy for?

> **Key Words**
>
> **Lactic acid**
> **Oxygen debt**
> **Aerobic zone**
> **Anaerobic capacity**

The Short- and Long-term Effects of Exercise

You must be able to:

- Explain the short-term effects of exercise
- Explain how the respiratory system and cardio-vascular system work together
- Explain the long-term effects of exercise.

The Short-term Effects of Exercise

Short-term effects: lactic acid accumulation and muscle fatigue

- Contraction of muscles occurs when any movement takes place.
- The temperature of muscles rises.
- Your muscles work harder during exercise, therefore more oxygen is required.
- If you cannot supply enough oxygen to your working muscles, you will accumulate lactic acid, feel pain and tire quickly.

Short-term effects: **heart rate**, stroke volume and **cardiac output**

- When you exercise your heart rate increases, as more oxygen is needed at the muscles.
- **Stroke volume** increases, allowing more blood to be pumped around the body.
- Blood pressure increases.
- Cardiac output increases.
- If you cannot supply enough oxygen to your working muscles, heart rate will remain high until the **oxygen debt** is fully recovered.

Short-term effects: depth and rate of breathing

- When you exercise more oxygen is required and your breathing rate will increase.
- The depth of your breathing also increases, therefore tidal volume increases and you consume more oxygen per breath.
- When you are working anaerobically, until you consume enough oxygen to meet the oxygen debt, your breathing rate and depth will remain high.

Respiratory and Cardio-vascular Systems Working Together

- The systems work together to allow participation in physical activity and sport and to help an athlete recover by getting oxygen to the working muscles.
- Oxygen is taken into the lungs.
- The oxygen is transferred to blood.
- Then it is transported to muscles.
- Then carbon dioxide is removed.

The Long-term Effects of Exercise on the Body's Systems

The muscular system

Adaptations occur to your body after long-term training.

- Muscles get bigger and stronger. This is called **hypertrophy**.
- Muscles are able to apply more force.
- The body's ability to endure lactic acid increases.

The respiratory system

- Chest muscles get stronger.
- Chest cavity becomes larger.
- Vital capacity increases.
- The body can supply more oxygen.
- Aerobic endurance will develop.

The cardio-vascular system

- The heart gets larger and stronger (cardiac hypertrophy).
- More force with each beat will occur.
- Stroke volume increases.
- Cardiac output increases.
- Lower resting heart rate.
- Blood vessels improve in physical shape and get stronger.
- Blood pressure decreases.

> ### Key Point
>
> Regular physical activity can result in adaptations to muscular, respiratory and circulatory systems. These potential changes can prepare the body better for strenuous activity.

Left ventricular hypertrophy

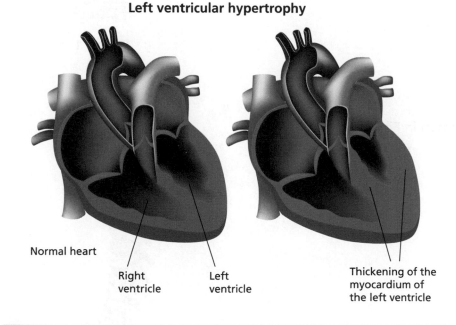

Normal heart

Right ventricle

Left ventricle

Thickening of the myocardium of the left ventricle

Quick Test

1. What happens to your muscles if you do not receive enough oxygen during exercise?
2. Blood pressure, cardiac output and stroke volume all increase when exercising. True or False?
3. State three long-term effects for the muscular, respiratory and cardio-vascular systems after exercise.

> ### Key Words
>
> Heart rate
> Stroke volume
> Oxygen debt
> Cardiac output

The Structure and Functions of the Musculo-skeletal System

1 What classification of bone is shown in Figure 1?

Tick (✓) one answer.

a) Long ( )

b) Short ( )

c) Irregular ( )

d) Flat ( )   [1]

Figure 1

2 What classification of bone is shown in Figure 2?

Tick (✓) one answer.

a) Long ( )

b) Short ( )

c) Irregular ( )

d) Flat ( )   [1]

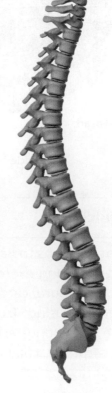

Figure 2

3 What classification of bone is shown in Figure 3?

Tick (✓) one answer.

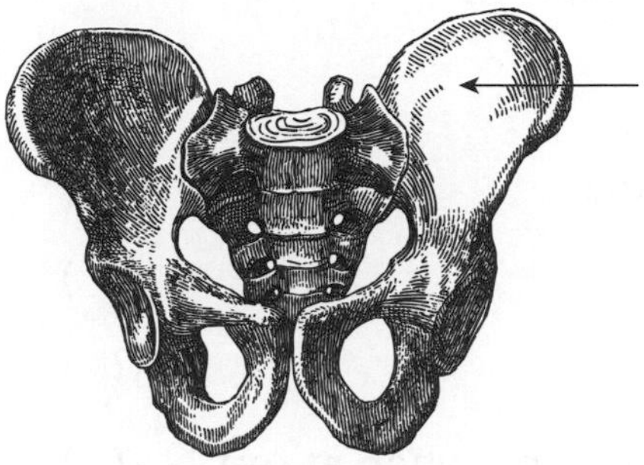

Figure 3

a) Long ( )

b) Short ( )

c) Irregular ( )

d) Flat ( ) [1]

4 Identify three functions of the skeleton.

[3]

5 Explain two different classifications of bones.

[2]

Total Marks .... / 8

The Structure and Functions of the Cardio-respiratory System

1 Which one of the following is the correct description for vital capacity?

Tick (✓) one answer.

a) The maximum amount of air that can be breathed in or out. ( )

b) The amount of times the heart beats in a minute. ( )

c) The amount of oxygen you need when exercising. ( )

d) The amount of air that enters the lungs during normal breathing when at rest. ( ) [1]

2 Which one of the following is the correct description for tidal volume?

Tick (✓) one answer.

a) The maximum amount of air that can be breathed in or out. ( )

b) The amount of times the heart beats in a minute. ( )

c) The amount of oxygen you need when exercising. ( )

d) The amount of air that enters the lungs during normal breathing when at rest. ( ) [1]

3 Explain the structure of alveoli and the process of gas exchange.

_____

_____

_____

_____

_____

_____ [3]

4 Which one of the following is the correct description for tidal volume? For an adult the average tidal volume is...

Tick (✓) one answer.

a) 500 ml ( )

b) 450 ml ( )

c) 5000 ml ( )

d) 50 ml ( ) [1]

5 Complete the following statement about the labelled structure of the cardio-respiratory system in Figure 4.

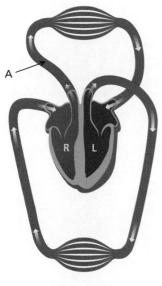

Figure 4

The structure labelled A in **Figure 4** is the _____.

The _____ takes blood with little _____ to the lungs.   [3]

6 Define heart rate.

_____

_____ [1]

7 Which one of the following is the correct answer? What is the painful, fatiguing by-product sometimes produced when working anaerobically?

Tick (✓) one answer.

a) Oxygen   ( )

b) Carbon dioxide   ( )

c) Lactic acid   ( )

d) Nitrogen   ( )   [1]

Total Marks _____ / 11

Practice Questions

Anaerobic and Aerobic Exercise

1 Explain adaptations to the muscular system.

_____

_____

_____

_____

_____

[3]

2 Explain adaptations to the respiratory system.

_____

_____

_____

_____

_____

_____

[3]

3 Explain adaptations to the cardio-vascular system.

_____

_____

_____

_____

_____

[3]

Total Marks _____ / 9

The Short- and Long-term Effects of Exercise

1 After undertaking long-term training your body will have a decrease in resting heart rate. Circle the correct answer.

True   False   [1]

2 Explain the short-term effects of exercise on heart rate, blood pressure, stroke volume and cardiac output.

Heart rate:

_____

_____ [1]

Blood pressure:

_____

_____ [1]

Stroke volume:

_____

_____ [1]

Cardiac output:

_____

_____ [1]

3 Which one of the following is not a short-term effect of exercise?

Tick (✓) one answer.

a) Blood pressure increases.   (   )

b) Heart rate increases.   (   )

c) Oxygen debt.   (   )

d) Muscles get bigger and stronger.   (   )   [1]

Total Marks _____ / 6

Lever Systems

You must be able to:

- Explain the different classifications of levers
- Identify the advantages and disadvantages of the body's levers.

Classification of Levers

There are three classes of lever: first class, second class and third class. The role of the fulcrum, the load and the effort determine the classification of each of the levers.

- **Fulcrum** – is the point of movement or pivot, generally at the centre of a joint.
- **Load** – is the body's weight or an external object.
- **Effort** – is a muscular force to move the load.

The three classes of lever are:

- first class – fulcrum in the middle
- second class – **resistance** in the middle
- third class – effort in the middle.

First class levers

- The fulcrum is between the effort and the load.
- Both effort and load are in the same direction.
- For this lever, the fulcrum lies between the effort and load.
- An example is the place where your skull (fulcrum) meets the top of your spine.
- Your skull is the lever and the neck muscles provide the force (effort) to lift your head up (load). When the neck muscles relax, your head nods forward.

Second class levers

- Fulcrum is at one end of the lever.
- Load is in the middle of the lever.
- Effort is at the opposite end of the lever to the fulcrum.
- The direction of effort is opposite the load.

> ### Key Point
>
> A lever always consists of three parts: fulcrum, load and effort. A lever must work in appropriate combination with the muscles and bones to enable movement at the leg or arm.

First class levers

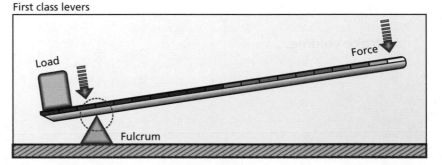

Second class levers

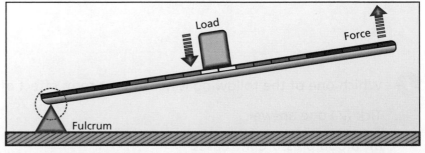

Third class levers

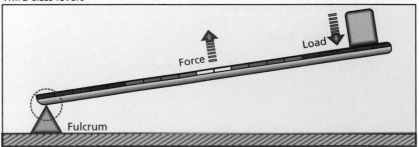

- An example of this is stepping up onto your toes – the fulcrum is at the toes.
  - The load is the body.
  - The effort is in the calf muscles pulling the body up onto the toes.
- Most effective lever as it can move a large weight, with little force.

Third class levers

- Fulcrum and load are at different ends of the lever.
- However, effort is off-centre of the lever near the fulcrum.
- Not as effective as second class levers.
- Small movements of the muscles create long lever movement.
- An example is the pivot at the elbow; the forearm acts as the lever arm.
- Bicep muscles provide the force and pull the forearm towards the upper arm.

Mechanical advantages and disadvantages of the body's lever systems

Class of lever	Advantages	Disadvantages
First class	• Strong • Stable • Increasing the length of the lever will increase the mechanical advantage	• Slow acting movement • Limited flexibility
Second class	• Strong • Stable • Increasing the length of the lever arm will increase the mechanical advantage	• Slow acting movement • Limited flexibility
Third class	• Large range of motion • Movement is fast • Increasing the length of the lever arm will decrease the mechanical advantage	• The amount of force applied must always exceed the weight of the load

Quick Test

1. What is the fulcrum?
2. What is the load?
3. What is the effort?
4. Explain and give examples of the three different types of levers.

Key Words

Fulcrum
Load
Effort
Resistance

Planes and Axes of Movement

You must be able to:

- Explain the body's planes of movement
- Explain the body's axes of movement
- Explain movement skills.

Movement Patterns Using Body Planes and Axes

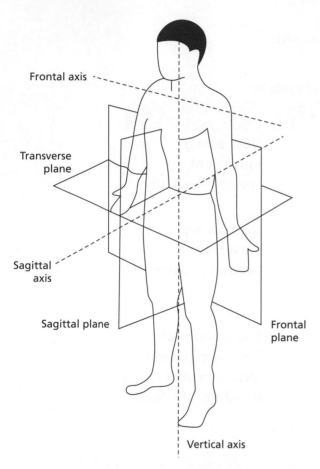

Frontal axis

Transverse plane

Sagittal axis

Sagittal plane

Frontal plane

Vertical axis

> ### Key Point
>
> Axes – an axis is a straight line around which an object rotates. Movement at a joint takes place in a plane about an axis.

- Sagittal **plane** – a vertical plane, which passes from front to rear separating the body into right and left parts.
- Frontal plane – passes from side to side at right angles to the sagittal plane, and separates the body into a front and back section.
- Transverse plane – a horizontal plane that separates the body into upper and lower parts.

There are three planes of motion in which we can move. The majority of our movements are not simply up and down, or side to side, particularly when we are participating in physical activity or sport. They are often a combination of movements in different planes.

Anatomical Neutral

This is the initial position for describing any movement pattern in physical activity or sport. It is essential to recognise what is meant by certain movement patterns.

Anatomical neutral is:
- Standing upright
- Legs together and knees straight
- Toes pointing straight forwards
- Arms by the sides
- Palms facing forwards

The Three Axes

- Frontal **axis** – bypasses from side to side at right angles to the sagittal plane.
- Sagittal axis – bypasses horizontally from front to rear lying at right angles to the frontal plane.
- Vertical axis – bypasses from head to foot at right angles to the transverse plane.

Sagittal plane–frontal axis movement
The **rotation** in a high board dive is an example of movement in the sagittal plane and around the frontal axis.

Frontal plane–sagittal axis movement
Rotation in a gymnastics cartwheel is an example of movement in the frontal plane about the sagittal axis.

Transverse plane–vertical axis movement
Movement in a full twist jump in trampolining is an example of movement in the transverse plane about the vertical axis.

Movement Skills

You need to know the various terms that can be used to describe sports movements, these include:
- Efficiency – using little effort and is effective.
- Predetermined – selected before the start.
- Coordinated – a well synchronised and effective movement.
- Fluent – smooth actions.
- Aesthetic – visually appealing, with no errors.

> **Key Point**
>
> Planes of movement – most bodily movements are not simply horizontal and vertical, therefore, to help explain dynamic movement, three imaginary lines are passed through the body to help explain movements occurring in each.

> **Quick Test**
>
> 1. What are the body's three planes of movement?
> 2. What are the body's axes of movement?
> 3. Name the axis and plane when an athlete undertakes rotation in a high board dive.

> **Key Words**
>
> Plane
> Anatomical neutral
> Axis
> Rotation

The Relationship between Health and Fitness

You must be able to:

- Explain the components of health-related fitness
- Explain the components of skill-related fitness.

The Components of Fitness

Health-related components of **fitness**

- Cardio-vascular fitness (aerobic endurance) is the ability to exercise the entire body for long periods of time.
- Strength is the amount of force a muscle can exert against a resistance.
- Muscular endurance is the ability to use voluntary muscles many times without getting tired.
- Flexibility is the range of movement possible at a joint or a series of joints.
- Body composition is the percentage of body weight that is fat, muscle and bone.

To participate in sport and physical activity, you need to have fitness that is relevant to the activity you are undertaking as well as a general level of underlying fitness, balanced in all components, whatever sport or physical activity you participate in. You also need to have the required skill proficiencies – this is called skill-related fitness.

Skill-related components of fitness

- Agility is the ability to change direction at speed. An example of a sport that uses agility is basketball, where the player must evade opponents.
- Balance is the ability to retain the centre of mass above the base of support when stationary (static balance) or moving (dynamic balance). Riding a bike is an activity that requires good balance.
- Coordination is the ability to use two or more body parts together. In gymnastics, using the beam is a good example of a discipline that requires coordination.
- Power is the ability to undertake strength performances quickly (power = strength × speed); participants in a rugby scrum need power that is a combination of speed and strength.
- Reaction time is the time between the presentation of a stimulus and the onset of movement. A sprinter moving away from the starting blocks after the starting pistol has been fired is an example of reaction time.

- Speed is how quickly a movement can be performed or a distance can be covered. A sprinter covering a 100-metre track in as little time as possible is an example of speed.

It is possible for you to be in good physical fitness whilst not being in good health. For example if you do not consume a healthy and nutritious diet, you will not receive the required macronutrients and micronutrients.

Key Points

- Fitness is the ability to meet the demands of the environment. Everybody needs to have a level of fitness for everyday activities.

- Health is the state of physical, mental and social well-being and takes into account injury and illness.

- Exercise is a form of physical activity which maintains and improves health and physical fitness.

- Performance is how well a physical task is completed.

- If you have good health-related fitness, you are healthy and able to successfully undertake everyday activities without feeling fatigue.

Quick Test

1. Define fitness and health.
2. Define exercise and performance.
3. List the five components of health-related fitness.
4. List the six components of skill-related fitness.

Key Words

Health
Fitness

Components of Fitness Data Interpretation 1

You must be able to:

- Understand the Cooper run test, Stork balance test, ruler drop reaction time test, Harvard step test and grip dynamometer test
- Interpret the results of the Cooper run test, Stork balance test, ruler drop reaction time test, Harvard step test and grip dynamometer test.

Fitness Tests

Cooper 12-minute run test
Measures cardio-vascular fitness (aerobic endurance) and can be carried out anywhere as long as you have a known distance and a stopwatch – but it is usually carried out at an athletics track. Participants try to run as far as they can in 12 minutes. The table below shows the normative **data** that can be interpreted to estimate fitness levels.

Data Interpretation

Cooper 12-minute run test

Age	Excellent	Above average	Average	Below average	Poor
Males 13–14	>2700 m	2400–2700 m	2200–2399 m	2100–2199 m	<2100 m
Females 13–14	>2000 m	1900–2000 m	1600–1899 m	1500–1599 m	<1500 m
Males 15–16	>2800 m	2500–2800 m	2300–2499 m	2200–2299 m	<2200 m
Females 15–16	>2100 m	2000–2100 m	1700-1999 m	1600–1699 m	<1600 m
Males 17–19	>3000 m	2700–3000 m	2500–2699 ftm	2300–2499 m	<2300 m
Females 17–19	>2300 m	2100–2300 m	1800–2099 m	1700–1799 m	<1700 m

Stork balance test
- The participant stands on one leg, raised onto the ball of the foot, without shoes on. The non-standing foot is positioned against the inside of the knee.
- The participant then raises the heel off the floor. Once the foot is off the floor time is recorded.
- The time stops when the participant fails to hold the required position.
- The table can then be used to assess balance.

Stork balance test

Rating	Score (seconds)
Excellent	>50
Good	40–50
Average	25–39
Fair	10–24
Poor	<10

Ruler drop reaction time test
- A non-participant holds a ruler in line with the participant's index finger and the thumb of their dominant hand. The zero centimetre line needs to be in line with the thumb.
- The non-participant drops the ruler.
- The participant catches the ruler.
- The distance on the ruler is recorded. This test is repeated twice.
- The average is then calculated.
- The table can then be used to assess flexibility.

Ruler drop reaction time test

Excellent	<7.5 cm
Above average	7.5–15.9 cm
Average	15.9–20.4 cm
Below average	20.4–28 cm
Poor	>28 cm

Harvard step test

Measures cardio-vascular fitness (aerobic endurance). The test protocols are as follows:

- test uses your recovery rate to assess your cardio-vascular fitness
- you need a gym bench, stopwatch and an assistant
- to complete the test you step on to a standard bench once every two seconds for five minutes (150 steps)
- the assistant checks pace
- one minute after finishing take your pulse (bpm) – this is pulse 1
- two minutes after finishing take your pulse again – this is pulse 2
- three minutes after finishing take your pulse for the final time – this is pulse 3
- use the formula below to determine your level of fitness
- compare to the normative data that follows for a 16-year-old athlete.

Measuring pulse

Normative data, 16-year-old athlete

Result = 30,000 ÷ (pulse 1 + pulse 2 + pulse 3)

Gender	Excellent	Above average	Average	Below average	Poor
Male	>90	80–90	65–79	55–64	<55
Female	>86	76–86	61–75	50–60	<50

Grip dynamometer test

This test measures strength.

- Weightlifting and rugby are two examples of sports that need good grip and strength.
- Using a dynamometer you can quickly and easily record forearm strength.
- By using the meter you can record a maximum reading (kg) from three attempts.

The data table below can be used to compare your results to normative results for 16–19 year-olds.

Dynamometer

Normative data, 16–19 year-olds

Gender	Excellent	Good	Average	Fair	Poor
Male	>56	51–56	45–50	39–44	<39
Female	>36	31–36	25–30	19–24	<19

> ### Quick Test
>
> 1. What component of fitness does the Cooper 12-minute run test measure?
> 2. What component of fitness does the Harvard step test measure?
> 3. What component of fitness does the grip dynamometer test measure?

Key Words

Fitness testing
Data
Normative data

Components of Fitness Data Interpretation 2

You must be able to:

- Understand 30-m sprint test, vertical jump test, rep max test, one-minute sit-up test and one-minute press-up test
- Interpret the results of 30-m sprint test, vertical jump test, sit and reach test, one-minute sit-up test and one-minute press-up test.

30-m sprint test

This test measures speed.

- Nearly all sports require an individual to move at speed.
- The aim of this test is to run as fast as you can over 30 metres, after a thorough warm-up.
- You will need an assistant, a stopwatch and cones.
- Your assistant will need to record the time it takes you to run 30 metres.

Data interpretation

Gender	Excellent	Above average	Average	Below average	Poor
Male	<4 seconds	4.0–4.2 seconds	4.3–4.4 seconds	4.5–4.6 seconds	>4.6 seconds
Female	<4.5 seconds	4.5–4.6 seconds	4.7–4.8 seconds	4.9–5.0 seconds	>5 seconds

Vertical jump test

This test identifies power.

- This test is used by coaches and athletes to measure an athlete's standing jump ability.
- It is important to remember to record the distance jumped – not the height jumped.

Rep max test

This test measures muscular strength.

- Participant will warm up.
- Participant will attempt to lift the heaviest weight they can in one single repetition.
- It is essential to allow plenty of rest between efforts, to make sure that the highest weight lifted is the true maximum.
- Maximum weight is recorded and can be used to assess maximal strength.

Sit and reach test

The sit and reach is a very common and simple test that measures the flexibility of your lower back and hamstrings.

Use the following table to compare your scores.

Sit and reach test

	Very poor	Poor	Fair	Average	Good	Excellent	Superior
Male	−20 cm +	−19 to −9 cm	−8 to −1 cm	0–5 cm	6–16 cm	17–26 cm	27 cm +
Female	−15 cm +	−14 to −8 cm	−7 to 0 cm	1–10 cm	11–20 cm	21–30 cm	30 cm +

One-minute sit-up test

This test measures muscular endurance.

- Rowing is an example of a sport that needs good muscular endurance as it is predominantly based on repeated contractions at a single joint.
- This test requires an individual to sit up as many times as they can in one minute.
- Simply count how many sit-ups you can do in one minute.

One-minute press-up test

This test measures muscular endurance.

- Cycling is an example of a sport that needs good muscular endurance as it is predominantly based on repeated contractions at a single joint.
- This test requires an individual to complete a press-up as many times as they can in one minute.
- Simply count how many press-ups you can do in one minute.

Normative data, 18–25 year-olds

Male 18–25	
Excellent	>49
Good	44–49
Above average	39–43
Average	35–38
Below average	31–34
Poor	25–30
Very poor	<24

Female 18–25	
Excellent	>43
Good	37–43
Above average	33–36
Average	29–32
Below average	25–28
Poor	18–24
Very poor	<18

Normative data, 18–25 year-olds

Male 18–25	
Excellent	>56
Good	47–56
Above average	35–46
Average	19–34
Below average	11–18
Poor	4–10
Very poor	<4

Female 18–25	
Excellent	>35
Good	27–35
Above average	21–26
Average	11–20
Below average	6–10
Poor	2–5
Very poor	<2

Key Point

Data interpretation is making sense of numerical data that has been collected and analysed.

Quick Test

1. What component of fitness does the vertical jump test measure?
2. What component of fitness does the sit and reach test measure?
3. What component of fitness does the 30-metre sprint test measure?

Key Words

Data interpretation

The Principles of Training 1

You must be able to:

- Explain the principles of training
- Explain how thresholds can be used to support training.

Training Principles and their Application

Planning training using the principles of training

Specificity

- Training needs to be specific to the activity.
- Training needs to focus on the same type of fitness component and muscle grouping.
- For example, sprinters do mostly speed training.
- Training needs to take into consideration an individual's physiological and psychological needs.

Progressive overload

- Gradual increases in intensity are required to create an overload and to progress.
- Training must be at a higher intensity than previously undertaken for the body to adapt.
- It is important to allow the body time to recover.

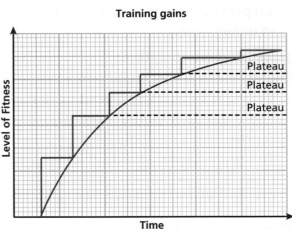

Training gains

FITT

- This increase can take place in four ways.
- Frequency – how often we train.
- Intensity – the amount of effort we put in.
- Type – the different methods of training that are used to increase effort.
- Time – increasing the duration of training sessions.

Overtraining

- If too much training is undertaken, it can result in poor performance, injury and illness.
- Overtraining can mean training adaptations do not occur.

Reversibility

- Training effects are reversible, if no further training is undertaken.

Thresholds of Training

Using the Karvonen formula

- Maximum heart rate can be used to predict if you are working aerobically or anaerobically.
- Calculate maximum heart rate by using: 220 – age = MHR.

> ### Key Points
>
> To improve the aerobic threshold:
> - heart rate needs to be in the aerobic target zone, which is 60–80%
> - aerobic endurance needs to be steady and not too fast (marathon runners use aerobic training).

- Using the Karvonen method resting heart is then subtracted from maximum heart rate; this gives maximum heart rate reserve.
- For example, Will, age 33, has a resting heart rate of 56 therefore his maximum heart rate reserve = 131.
- If Will wanted to train at 60% he would need to multiply his maximum heart rate reserve (131) × 0.6 = 81 + resting heart rate (56) = 135.
- This can then be used to calculate training zones for Will.

Training zone percentage	Heart rate
50%	122
60%	135
70%	148
80%	161
90%	174

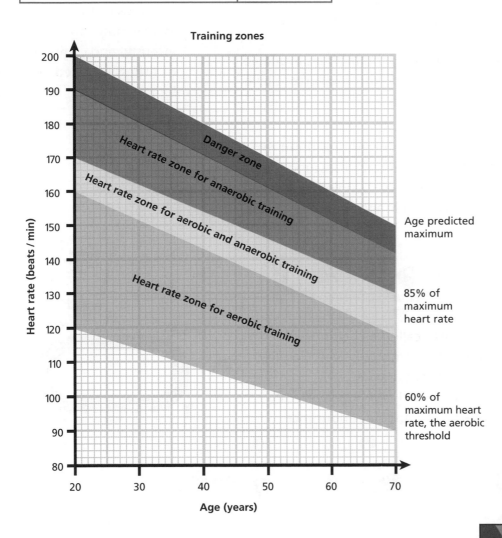

Training zones

Key Points

To improve the anaerobic threshold:

- heart rate needs to be in the anaerobic target zone, which is 80%–90%
- anaerobic exercise needs to be performed in short, fast bursts where the heart cannot supply enough oxygen to the muscles
- anaerobic training improves the ability of the muscles to work without oxygen (sprinters use anaerobic training).

Quick Test

1. How can you predict maximum heart rate?
2. What is the target zone for aerobic exercise?
3. What is the target zone for anaerobic exercise?

Key Words

Specificity
Progressive overload
Overtraining
Reversibility

The Principles of Training 2

You must be able to:

- Explain how to choose training methods
- Identify levels of training intensity
- Explain the advantages and disadvantages of different training methods.

Choosing Training Methods and Intensities

- It is important to choose a method of training that develops the appropriate component of fitness.
- The intensity of training should meet the aims of the individual session and the demands of the required different physical activities or sports.
- Methods of training can be determined by the facilities available.
- Intensity of training must also correspond with the current level of fitness.

Training methods for specific components
- Continuous – working at sustained aerobic intensity without rest for a minimum of 20 minutes; this improves cardio-vascular fitness.
- **Fartlek** – or 'speed play' training incorporates changing your speed, terrain or intensity. Fartlek improves aerobic and anaerobic fitness.

> **Key Point**
>
> Methods of training ideally match the intensity and components of fitness required by an individual.

10 min jog → 100 m walk → 50 m sprint → 5 min jog → …and so on

- **Circuits** – involve a series of exercises called a circuit. Each activity takes place at a 'station'. It can improve speed, agility, coordination, balance and muscular endurance.
- **Intervals** – period of work and relief with varying levels of intensity. Used to develop speed and muscular endurance.

25 m sprint → 30 sec rest → 25 m sprint → 30 sec rest → …and so on

- **Plyometric** – muscles are used to exert maximum force in short periods of time, with the aim of developing speed and strength (power). Examples include bounding, jumping and hopping.
- Weight training – uses weights to provide resistance. Used to develop muscular strength. By varying weight, sets and reps, different goals can be achieved. Muscular endurance, muscular strength and power can all be developed.

Advantages and disadvantages of different training methods

	Component of fitness	Advantages	Disadvantages
Body Pump • Focuses on eight different muscle groups • Combines weight training and aerobics	Develops strength and cardio-vascular endurance	• Develops strength and cardio-vascular endurance • Targets specific muscle groups • High intensity	• Instructor cannot give significant individual support • Poor technique is not always corrected and can lead to injury
Aerobics • Exercising to music in a group fitness class • Working your body aerobically	Develops strength, flexibility and cardio-vascular endurance	• Develops flexibility and cardio-vascular endurance • Good for weight loss • Improves coordination • High intensity	• Can be high impact on body joints
Pilates/yoga • Completing a variety of stretches and exercises • Pilates often focuses on the core muscles and the full body • Used for body conditioning	Strength and flexibility	• Develops strength and flexibility • Targets specific muscle groups • Improves coordination	• Stretches can be very challenging • Stretches incorrectly performed, by not using the technique demonstrated, can lead to injury
Spinning • Group high intensity exercise class using bikes • Resistance and intensity can be set to different individual levels	Cardio-vascular fitness and anaerobic fitness	• Develops cardio-vascular endurance • Can develop the athlete both aerobically and anaerobically • High intensity	• Upper body has very little adaptation • Not much variety • Can be uncomfortable

Quick Test

1. What components of fitness does a Body Pump class use?
2. Name a disadvantage of an aerobics class.
3. What is the minimum number of minutes an individual should train for continuous training to be effective?

Key Words

Fartlek
Circuits
Intervals
Plyometric

The Long-term Effects of Exercise

You must be able to:

- Explain long-term training effects
- Explain the benefits of long-term training to the skeletal system and the cardio-respiratory system.

The Long-term Effects of Exercise

Long-term training effects

- Train for longer and more intensely.
- Fitness levels are improved.
- Motor development skills are improved.
- Recovery is quicker.
- Sleep better.
- Resting heart rate is lower (bradycardia).
- Blood pressure is lower.
- Reduced body fat.
- Improved health.

Benefits to the musculo-skeletal system

- Increased bone density – making bones stronger and more able to withstand potential impacts better. Additionally, increased bone density can positively enable an individual to have a more active lifestyle in later life.
- Increased strength of ligaments and tendons – improving joint stability, articular cartilage increases.
- Muscle hypertrophy – muscles become bigger in size, fibres get thicker and stronger. When taking part in physical activity and sport you will be able to apply more force and strength to movement. Stronger and thicker muscles potentially fatigue less, thus reducing the chances of injury.

The importance of rest for adaptations to take place

- Without adequate rest, changes will not occur. Rest is a crucial part of any training programme and is often neglected by both amateur and professional athletes. To achieve long-term physiological improvements to either the musculo-skeletal system or cardio-respiratory system rest needs to occur.
- It is important to allow adequate time to recover before the next training session.

Key Point

Long-term training effects are changes in the body that usually occur over a prolonged period of training.

Benefits to the cardio-respiratory system

- Decreased resting heart rate – as your heart becomes stronger and more efficient more blood is pumped per beat, so resting heart rate is reduced.
- Faster recovery – after long-term training athletes are able to recover more quickly.
- Increased resting stroke volume – more blood is pumped per heart beat.
- Increased maximum cardiac output – more blood is pumped per minute.
- Increased size/strength of heart – the heart becomes bigger and stronger.
- Increased capillarisation – a greater network of capillaries is created to assist respiration.
- Increase in number of **red blood cells** – this helps with oxygen transfer to the working muscles.
- Drop in resting blood pressure – due to more elastic muscular wall of veins and arteries.
- Increased **lung capacity**/volume and vital capacity – this means you breathe in more oxygen because the bigger the capacity, the more air comes in.
- Increased number of alveoli – results in more efficient gaseous exchange.
- Increased strength of diaphragm and external intercostal muscles – results in greater force and less likelihood of feeling fatigued.

Quick Test

1. Name the long-term effects of training.
2. Explain the effects of long-term training on the musculo-skeletal system.
3. Explain the long-term effects of training on the cardio-respiratory system.

How to Optimise Training and Prevent Injury

You must be able to:

- Explain what a pre-activity readiness questionnaire is
- Explain potential hazards
- Explain common sporting injuries and methods to prevent injuries
- Explain the effects of performance-enhancing drugs.

Using a Pre-Activity Readiness Questionnaire (PARQ)

- Screening questionnaire, to be used before starting exercise.
- To identify possible risk of undertaking exercise.
- Constructed using responses to the questions.
- Identifies individuals who need to seek further medical advice and recommendations can be made.

Potential Hazards

Sports halls and fitness centres	Playing fields and artificial surfaces	Swimming pools
<ul><li>Emergency exits</li><li>Inappropriate footwear</li><li>Building faults/no safety padding</li><li>Collisions, slips, trips and falls</li><li>Hazardous substances</li><li>Poor manual handling</li></ul>	<ul><li>Slippery, dry or damaged surfaces</li><li>Drains</li><li>Debris</li><li>External objects on field of play</li><li>Field equipment from other sports, such as backstops, football sleds, infields</li><li>Potential abrasions</li></ul>	<ul><li>Risk of drowning</li><li>Hard to view areas</li><li>Slips, trips and falls</li><li>Ladder access</li><li>Changes in floor</li></ul>

Injuries

Prevent **injury** through:

- using the principles of training
- following the rules and regulations
- using the appropriate protective clothing and equipment
- checking equipment and facilities before use
- warming up and cooling down.

Injuries that can occur in physical activity and sport

Concussion

- Usually due to direct impact to the head.
- There is a loss of consciousness.
- Episodes of memory loss and distorted sight.
- Confusion, slow response to questioning.

Fracture

* Broken or cracked bone/s.

Dislocation

* One of the bones at a joint is knocked out of place.

Sprain

* Ligaments become stretched at a joint.

Torn cartilage

* Damage to the surface area of the cartilage between bones.

Abrasion

* Damage to the surface of the skin.

Performance-enhancing Drugs (PEDs)

	Advantages	Disadvantages
Anabolic steroids	• Build muscle • Train harder	• Potential mood swings/anger • Damage to kidneys
Beta blockers	• More efficient heart • Relaxes and reduces tension • Lower blood pressure • Improve fine control	• Depression • Sleep loss • Dizziness, fatigue
Diuretics	• Used to remove fluid • Aid weight loss • Masking agent	• Dehydration
Narcotic analgesics	• Reduces pain • Helps prevent fatigue	• Addictive
Growth hormones (GH)	• Build muscle mass • Ability to train longer	• Unusual growth • Heart problems • Diabetes • Arthritis
Stimulants	• Increased alertness • Resistance to fatigue	• Lead to addiction • Heart problems/attack
Blood doping	• Increased oxygen-carrying capacity	• Heart failure • Kidney problems
Erythropoietin (EPO)	• Increased red blood cells • Increased oxygen capacity	• Heart problems • Stroke

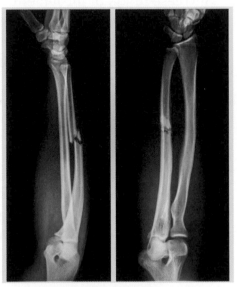

Example of a fracture

> ### Quick Test
>
> 1. What does PARQ stand for?
> 2. How can sports injuries be prevented?
> 3. Name five different types of performance-enhancing drugs.

Effective Use of Warm-up and Cool Down

You must be able to:

- Explain the effective use of a warm-up
- Explain the effective use of a cool down.

Warm-up and Cool Down

The aim of a warm-up is to prepare the body for exercise. Warm-ups:

- improve the elasticity of ligaments and tendons
- increase range of movement
- increase the temperature of muscles
- increase blood flow and amount of oxygen to the working muscles
- prepare the body for specific exercise/familiarisation
- prevent injuries
- enhance the person's ability to perform both physically and mentally.

The aim of a cool down is to:

- remove lactic acid
- prevent Delayed Onset of Muscle Soreness (**DOMS**)
- reduce the chance of fainting or dizziness
- maintain and develop flexibility through stretching
- reduce muscle temperature
- allow the heart to return to its resting rate
- help the body's transition back to a resting state/recover
- circulate blood and oxygen
- gradually reduce breathing rate
- increase removal of waste products such as lactic acid/CO_2
- aid recovery by stretching muscles
- maintain elevated breathing and heart rate, e.g. walk, jog
- allow a gradual reduction in intensity.

The stages of warm-up and their significance

	Activity	Reason
Stage 1	Light running/jogging/specific pulse raising for activity	• Increase heart rate • Increase blood flow • Raise muscle and body temperature
Stage 2	**Dynamic stretching**	• Improve movement patterns and range
Stage 3	Practice activities for specific activity	• Warms up relevant muscle groups
Stage 4	Mental preparation	• Visualise a good performance

Key Point

The pulse raiser is the initial stage of warm-up to various activities, and can be used to steadily raise the heart rate.

Activities in Warm-up and Cool Down

- Stage 1 – jogging/specific pulse-raising activity/pulse-raising fun game. For example, a long distance runner might complete a light jog, or for a primary school lesson children might play cat and mouse.
- Stage 2 – dynamic stretching. A long distance runner would complete a series of dynamic leg stretches incorporating the arms and core.
- Stage 3 – practice activities. This could be a runner completing a series of accelerating shuttle runs or a basketball player passing the ball backwards and forwards with a partner for 3 minutes.
- Stage 4 – mental preparation. This could be focusing on the game or discussing strategies and tactics.
- Dynamic stretching is best used to prepare for physical activity as it is able to re-create specific movement patterns that are required.
- **Static stretching** is best performed after exercise or physical activity to develop flexibility.

Static stretching
- A way to increase flexibility.
- Stretch is held (isometric) for up to 30 seconds.
- It is important to always do this safely and not overstretch.

PNF stretching (Proprioceptive Neuromuscular Facilitation)
- PNF stretching is used predominately for developing flexibility and is often used by gymnasts.
- Use of muscle contraction before the stretch in an attempt to achieve maximum muscle relaxation.
- Holding stretches to their maximum point and then relaxing.
- Repeating this between two and five times.
- Holding stretches for a minimum of 30 seconds.
- Areas that frequently cause individual sports people problems include the gastrocnemius/stretch soleus, hamstrings, quadriceps and adductors.

> ### Key Point
>
> Stretching is an essential stage of any warm-up programme. It needs to be completed after the initial pulse raiser – at this point the muscles are warm and more pliable.

Static cool down stretch

> ### Quick Test
>
> 1. State the aims of a warm-up.
> 2. State the aims of a cool down.
> 3. What are the four stages of a warm-up?

> ### Key Word
>
> DOMS
> **Dynamic stretching**
> **Static stretching**

Use of Data

You must be able to:

- Develop knowledge and understanding of data analysis in relation to key areas of physical activity and sport
- Demonstrate an understanding of how data is collected in fitness, physical and sports activities, using both quantitative and qualitative methods.

Quantitative and Qualitative Research

Quantitative research:
- formal and objective
- a methodical process
- numerical data is used to obtain and analyse information
- identifies similarities and relationships.

Qualitative research:
- subjective
- uses words rather than data
- looks at individual personal views
- attempts to explain why, rather than what or how many.

Types of Data

Primary data
- collected through questionnaires, interviews and observation
- used to investigate research problems.

Secondary data
- previously published data found.

Present data

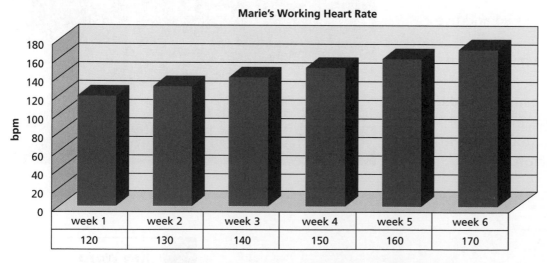

Marie's Working Heart Rate

	week 1	week 2	week 3	week 4	week 5	week 6
	120	130	140	150	160	170

Marie, who is 30, has a resting heart rate of 70 bpm and has just completed a six-week personal body pump exercise programme. The following table shows Marie's working heart rate during each week of her training. Her maximum heart rate is 190, using the simple maximum heart rate formula.

Marie's exercise programme showing max HR achieved

	Heart rate	Calculation 220–30 (age) = MHR 190	% Max HR	Aerobic or anaerobic
Week 1	120	120 working HR/190 MHR × 100 =	63%	Aerobic
Week 2	130	130 working HR/190 MHR × 100 =	68%	Aerobic
Week 3	140	140 working HR/190 MHR × 100 =	73%	Aerobic
Week 4	150	150 working HR/190 MHR × 100 =	78%	Aerobic
Week 5	160	160 working HR/190 MHR × 100 =	84%	Anaerobic
Week 6	170	170 working HR/190 MHR × 100 =	89%	Anaerobic

Cooper 12-minute run test results analysis

The table below shows normative data for the Cooper 12-minute run test.

Age	Excellent	Above average	Average	Below average	Poor
Males 13–14	>2700 m	2400–2700 m	2200–2399 m	2100–2199 m	<2100 m
Females 13–14	>2000 m	1900–2000 m	1600–1899 m	1500–1599 m	<1500 m
Males 15–16	>2800 m	2500–2800 m	2300–2499 m	2200–2299 m	<2200 m
Females 15–16	>2100 m	2000–2100 m	1700–1999 m	1600–1699 m	<1600 m
Males 17–19	>3000 m	2700–3000 m	2500–2699 m	2300–2499 m	<2300 m
Females 17–19	>2300 m	2100–2300 m	1800-2099 m	1700–1799 m	<1700 m

Three different people have completed the cardio-vascular endurance test. Their results represent different levels of fitness.

- Iris completed 2809 metres, she is a 15-year-old female, her result is classed as excellent.
- Edith completed 1908 metres, she is a 13-year-old female, her result is classed as above average.
- David completed 2202 metres, he is an 18-year-old male, his result is classed as poor.

> **Key Point**
>
> For any question using graphs or data you will need to use the information displayed in your answer and then comment on it in relation to normative data.

Quick Test

1. What is quantitative research?
2. What is qualitative research?
3. Analyse the results of the Cooper 12-minute run test above.

> **Key Words**
>
> Quantitative research
> Qualitative research

Lever Systems

1 Which of the following best describes a first class lever system?

Tick (✓) one answer.

a) The load and the fulcrum are at the same level on the lever. ( )

b) The load is in the middle. ( )

c) The fulcrum is in the middle of the lever. ( )

d) The load is at the right-hand end of the lever. ( )   [1]

2 Which of the following best describes a third class lever system?

Tick (✓) one answer.

a) The load and the fulcrum are at the same level on the lever. ( )

b) The load is in the middle. ( )

c) The effort is in the middle of the lever. ( )

d) The load is at the right-hand end of the lever. ( )   [1]

3 Explain two disadvantages of first class levers.

_____

_____

_____

_____   [2]

Total Marks _____ / 4

Planes and Axes of Movement

1 The plane is represented by the square.

The axis is represented by the dotted line.

Identify the plane and axis shown in **Figure 1**.

Tick (✓) one answer.

a) Transverse plane and vertical axis ( )

b) Frontal plane and vertical axis ( )

c) Transverse plane and frontal axis ( )

d) Sagittal plane and frontal axis ( ) [1]

Figure 1

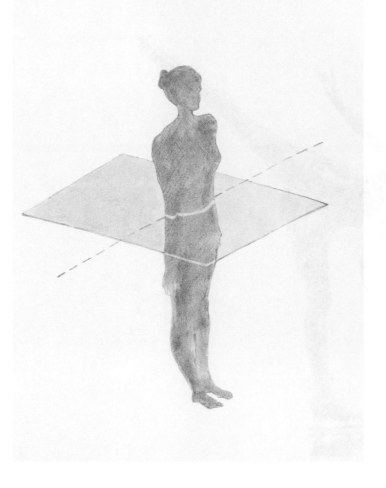

2 Analyse, using one example, how one of the ball and socket joints in the body allows the ice skater to complete the rotation.

_____

_____

_____

_____

_____

_____

_____

_____ [3]

Total Marks .... / 4

The Relationship between Health and Fitness

1 Define fitness, health and exercise.

Fitness:

_____

_____ [1]

Health:

_____

_____ [1]

Exercise:

_____

_____ [1]

2 Identify the five health-related components of fitness.

_____

_____

_____

_____

_____

_____ [5]

Total Marks _____ / 8

Components of Fitness Data Interpretation

Cooper run test

Measures cardiovascular fitness (aerobic endurance) and is usually carried out at an athletics track.

Age	Excellent	Above average	Average	Below average	Poor
Males 13–14	>2700 m	2400–2700 m	2200–2399 m	2100–2199 m	<2100 m
Females 13–14	>2000 m	1900–2000 m	1600–1899 m	1500–1599 m	<1500 m
Males 15–16	>2800 m	2500–2800 m	2300–2499 m	2200–2299 m	<2200 m
Females 15–16	>2100 m	2000–2100 m	1700–1999 m	1600–1699 m	<1600 m
Males 17–19	>3000 m	2700–3000 m	2500–2699 m	2300–2499 m	<2300 m
Females 17–19	>2300 m	2100–2300 m	1800–2099 m	1700–1799 m	<1700 m

Using the table above identify the correct level of fitness for the following individuals.
Tick (✓) one answer for each question.

1 Kelley is a 19-year-old female who runs 2456 metres.

    a) Excellent   ( )

    b) Above average   ( )

    c) Average   ( )

    d) Poor   ( )   **[1]**

2 Lewis is a 14-year-old male who runs 1456 metres.

    a) Excellent   ( )

    b) Above average   ( )

    c) Average   ( )

    d) Poor   ( )   **[1]**

3 Eddie is a 15-year-old male who runs 2456 metres.

    a) Excellent   ( )

    b) Above average   ( )

    c) Average   ( )

    d) Poor   ( )   **[1]**

Total Marks _____ / 3

The Principles of Training

1 Explain the principle of overload.

_____

_____

_____

_____

_____

_____

_____

_____ [4]

2 Explain the principle of reversibility.

_____

_____

_____

_____ [2]

3 Explain the principles of training specificity.

_____

_____

_____

_____

_____

_____ [3]

Total Marks _____ / 9

The Long-term Effects of Exercise

1 Identify the long-term effects of training on the musculo-skeletal system.

_____

_____

_____

_____

_____

_____

_____

_____ [3]

2 Identify the long-term effects of training on the cardio-vascular system.

_____

_____

_____

_____

_____

_____ [3]

3 Which one of the following best describes muscle hypertrophy?

Tick (✓) one answer.

a) Bone density increases.   ( )

b) Increased strength of ligaments and tendons.   ( )

c) Muscles become bigger in size, fibres get thicker and stronger. ( )

d) Increased cardiac output.   ( )   [1]

4 Identify the long-term effects of training on the respiratory system.

_____

_____

_____

_____

_____

_____ [3]

5 After undertaking long-term training your body will have a decrease in resting heart rate. Circle one answer.

True   False   [1]

6 After undertaking long-term training your body will recover more slowly. Circle one answer.

True   False   [1]

7 After undertaking long-term training your body will have an increased number of red blood cells. Circle one answer.

True   False   [1]

8 After undertaking long-term training your body will have reduced body fat. Circle one answer.

True   False   [1]

Total Marks _____ / 14

Practice Questions

How to Optimise Training and Prevent Injury

1 Explain how injuries can be prevented in sport.

_____

_____

_____

_____

_____

_____

_____ **[3]**

2 Explain what a sprain is.

_____

_____ **[1]**

Total Marks _____ / 4

Effective Use of Warm-up and Cool Down

1 Identify three reasons for a warm-up.

_____

_____

_____ **[3]**

Total Marks _____ / 3

Use of Data

1 Thomas, who is a 13-year-old male, runs 2105 metres in 12 minutes.

Age	Excellent	Above Average	Average	Below Average	Poor
Males 13–14	>2700 m	2400–2700 m	2200–2399 m	2100–2199 m	<2100 m
Females 13–14	>2000 m	1900–2000 m	1600–1899 m	1500–1599 m	<1500 m
Males 15–16	>2800 m	2500–2800 m	2300–2499 m	2200–2299 m	<2200 m
Females 15–16	>2100 m	2000–2100 m	1700–1999 m	1600–1699 m	<1600 m
Males 17–19	>3000 m	2700–3000 m	2500–2699 m	2300–2499 m	<2300 m
Females 17–19	>2300 m	2100–2300 m	1800–2099 m	1700–1799 m	<1700 m

Using the table, identify Thomas's current level of cardio-vascular fitness and explain methods that could be used to develop this.

[4]

2 Ruth, who is an 18-year-old female, runs 3305 metres in 12 minutes. She is classed as average on the Cooper 12-minute run test results analysis above.

Circle one answer.

True   False   [1]

Total Marks _____ / 5

Review Questions

The Structure and Functions of the Musculo-skeletal System

1 Match the correct description.

Tendon	When muscles contract, they exert this on bones.
Force	These attach muscles to bones.
Ligaments	Connect bones to bones. They are very strong.

[3]

2 Match the correct joint description.

Fixed	Joints contain a membrane that surrounds a joint, which contains synovial fluid; an example would be the hip.
Slightly moveable	Have no space between the bones, therefore no movement is possible, for example the skull.
Freely moveable	Joints are separated by cartilage and allow small amounts of movement, for example the vertebral column.

[3]

3 Complete the table on muscle fibres.

	Type I	Type IIa	Type IIx
Presence of oxygen			
Colour			
Speed of contraction			
Resistance to fatigue: high/medium/low			
Give a sporting example			

[5]

Total Marks _____ / 11

The Structure and Functions of the Cardio-respiratory System

1 Identify the correct movement patterns.

Movement pattern	Description	Tick (✓) the correct response
Is this flexion or extension?	The left knee is straightening.	Flexion ☐ Extension ☐
Is this adduction or abduction?	The arms are moving away from the midline of the body.	Abduction ☐ Adduction ☐
Is this rotation or circumduction?	 The shoulder is moving in a circular motion.	Rotation ☐ Circumduction ☐
Is this plantar-flexion or dorsiflexion?	Going up on to tip toes.	Plantar-flexion ☐ Dorsiflexion ☐

[4]

2 Explain the stages of inhalation and exhalation.

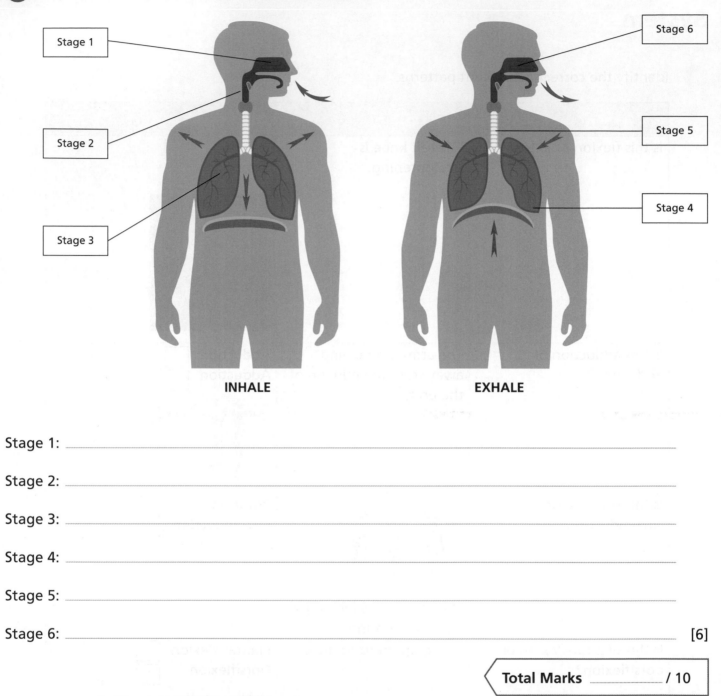

INHALE   EXHALE

Stage 1: _____

Stage 2: _____

Stage 3: _____

Stage 4: _____

Stage 5: _____

Stage 6: _____ [6]

Total Marks _____ / 10

Anaerobic and Aerobic Exercise

1 Some cells in your body do not require energy to function.

Circle the correct answer. [1]

True   False

2 Glucose is the fuel in your body that provides energy.

Circle the correct answer. [1]

True   False

3 When your body is not able to use oxygen lactic acid is made as a by-product, which is painful and causes fatigue.

Circle the correct answer. [1]

True   False

4 When exercising aerobically it is important for your heart rate to be operating at 50–70% of your maximum heart rate.

Circle the correct answer. [1]

True   False

Total Marks _____ / 4

The Short- and Long-term Effects of Exercise

1 Identify the body's energy sources.

_____

_____

_____ [3]

Total Marks _____ / 3

Physical, Emotional and Social Health, Fitness and Well-being

You must be able to:

- Explain the terms physical, emotional and social health
- Explain methods that can improve health.

Physical Health

Physical health is affected by various factors:

- individual biological make-up
- the environment you live in
- lifestyle and access to healthcare.

Physical health can be improved by:

- developing physical fitness (cardio-vascular fitness)
- losing weight (body composition)
- healthy diet
- managing stress, stopping smoking and not drinking alcohol.

> ### Key Point
>
> **Health** is a state of whole **physical**, mental and **social** well-being, with the absence of disease, illness or injury.

Emotional Health

Individuals who have good **emotional** health are:

- in control of their emotions
- adapt to change and deal with challenges
- have positive relationships.

Emotional health can be improved through:

- undertaking physical activity and managing stress
- getting enough rest and sleep
- good nutrition, limiting alcohol and avoiding cigarettes.

Social Health

Is the ability to form positive relationships with others and the capability to adjust easily to various social situations and behave fittingly.

Physical activity and sport can improve social health by:

- improving self esteem and empathy
- developing an understanding of better nutrition
- developing leadership skills.

Benefits are achieved by:

- making you feel better and reducing stress
- improved diet.

How to Promote Personal Health

The best results are achieved through a variety of methods and using the principles of training.

Training principles
- Specificity – training must be coordinated to the requirements of the activity. Specific to the individual in terms of personal fitness levels and personal goals.
- Progression – steadily increase intensity of activity and keep overloading. Progressing too quickly can lead to illness, injury or overtraining.
- Overload – gains are only made in fitness when training is more demanding than previously undertaken. Adaptations occur when you work harder than before. Overload can be completed by using the FITT principle.
- **Frequency** – how often, **intensity** – how hard, **time** – duration of training and the **type**.

Developing a Training Programme

When developing a **training programme**, the following FITT principles should be applied:
- frequency – how often to train per week
- intensity – how hard to train
- time – duration of training sessions – also the time for the whole programme such as how many weeks in length
- type – decide which type of training to use.

Monitoring
Monitoring your exercise programme is a way of evaluating progress. Required alterations can be made to training. Adjustments can be made to make sure that improvements occur and that individuals are being challenged, not overtrained. There are many methods that can be used to evaluate performance, these include:
- heart rate monitor – used to evaluate percentage of MHR
- training diary – individuals can record how they felt during training and adapt training as required
- testing – comparing test scores with initial results and normative data is an effective method to monitor progress
- feedback – from coaches/mentors/teachers can be used to adjust performance.

Key Words

Health
Physical
Social
Emotional
Training programme

The Consequences of a Sedentary Lifestyle 1

You must be able to:

- Explain lifestyle choices
- Explain the positive and negative impacts of lifestyle choices on health, fitness and well-being.

Lifestyle Factors

Diet

- A healthy diet can make you look and feel your best.
- Enable optimal sporting performance.
- Reduce the risk of getting many major diseases, including cancer, heart disease and diabetes.

Activity level

- As part of a healthy lifestyle adults need to do two types of physical activity each week: aerobic and strength exercises.
- According to government recommendations young people should undertake 60 minutes of physical activity every day.
- Adults should undertake 150 minutes of physical activity every week and strength exercises twice a week.

Consequences of a sedentary lifestyle

- Weight gain/obesity
- Heart disease
- Hypertension
- Diabetes
- Poor sleep
- Poor self esteem
- Lethargy.

Work/rest/sleep balance

- Satisfactory work, rest and sleep balance is essential for a person's health and well-being.
- Not enough sleep increases the probability of becoming ill.
- School-age children should sleep for 9–11 hours.
- Teenagers should sleep for 8–10 hours.
- Adults should sleep for 7–9 hours.

Recreational drugs

- Drug misuse can be harmful to your health.
- Possibly lead to addiction, anxiety/mood changes, depression, schizophrenia and other serious health issues, or even death.

Alcohol

- Consuming too much alcohol can increase your risk of getting a major disease, such as cancer, liver disease, stroke and mental health problems.

> **Key Point**
>
> Individuals can be fit but not necessarily healthy. A healthy individual is someone who is free from disease and infection.

Nicotine
- Smoking and the inhalation of nicotine increases your risk of developing many cancers and lung diseases.

Positive and negative impacts of lifestyle choices on health, fitness and well-being

	Positive impacts	Negative impacts
Diet	Good diet • Optimal sport performance • Maintain body weight • Improved health	Bad diet • Increases risk of coronary heart disease • Diabetes • High blood pressure • Poor physical fitness • Joint pain
Activity level	Undertaking physical activity • Reduces the risk of major illnesses, including heart disease, stroke, diabetes and cancer • Lowers the risk of early death by up to 30%	Not undertaking physical activity • Increases likelihood of gaining body weight • Increases blood pressure • Decreases bone strength • Increases stress • Lose flexibility • Lose muscle tone • Lose fitness • Lose strength
Work/rest/sleep balance	Good balance of work/rest/sleep • Allows the body to recover/repair and adapt	Poor balance of work/rest/sleep • Increases tiredness and the chances of becoming ill or injured
Recreational drugs	No positives	• Possibly lead to addiction, anxiety/mood changes, depression and schizophrenia • Other serious health issues, including death
Alcohol	No positives	• Increases chances of cancer, liver disease, stroke and mental health problems
Nicotine	No positives	• Increases your risk of developing many cancers and lung diseases

Quick Test

1. Identify three positive impacts of maintaining a good diet.
2. Apart from diet identify five other lifestyle factors.
3. Having sufficient sleep means the body will recover better from intensive exercise. True or False?

Key Words

Lifestyle
Consequences

The Consequences of a Sedentary Lifestyle 2

You must be able to:

- Explain the consequences of being overweight
- Identify trends in physical health data.

The Consequences of Being Overweight

- If you eat **more** calories than you use, your weight will **increase**.
- If you eat **fewer** calories than you use, your weight will **decrease**.
- Not eating enough calories will result in a lack of energy.
- Being **overweight** is not necessarily an issue. For example a great deal of heavy muscle is required by an American Football player.
- Being over-fat is having excess amounts of body fat.
- **Obese** is the official term for being over-fat.

Increased risks of:

- depression
- coronary heart disease
- high blood pressure
- diabetes
- increased risk of osteoporosis
- loss of muscle tone
- poor posture
- poor physical fitness.

Data Interpretation: trends in physical health issues

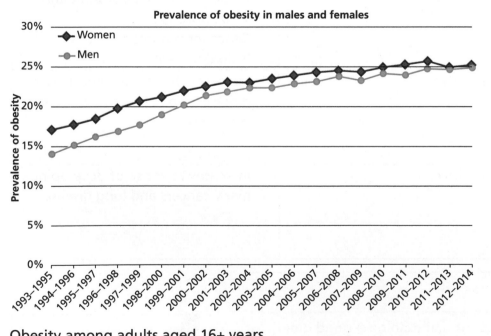

Obesity among adults aged 16+ years
- Obesity overall has been increasing since 1995.
- Obesity for men and women has increased since 1995.

Normal Artery

Fatty deposits can cause heart related issues

- Since 2013 obesity amongst women has marginally declined.
- Over 25% of men and women are obese.

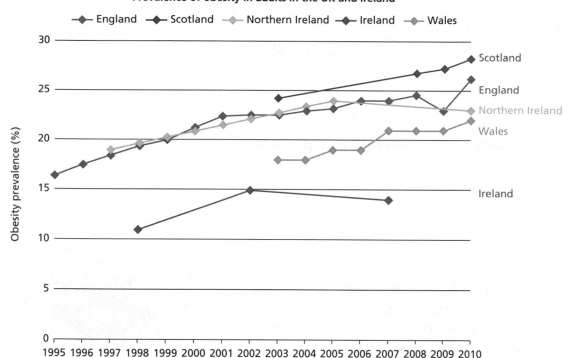

Prevalence of obesity in adults in the UK and Ireland

England ◆ Scotland ◆ Northern Ireland ◆ Ireland ◆ Wales

Trends in adult obesity in the UK and Ireland
- Obesity in the UK and Ireland over a 15-year period is increasing.
- Obesity is highest in Scotland.
- Obesity is lowest in Ireland.
- Heart and circulatory disease causes more than a quarter of all deaths in the UK.
- Around a quarter of adults in the UK are obese and in addition more than a third are overweight (using BMI).
- Around 30% of children in the UK are overweight or obese.
- One-third of men and nearly half of women in England do not achieve the recommended levels of physical activity.

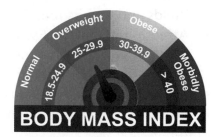

BODY MASS INDEX

BMI
There are different categories of being overweight. Body mass index (BMI) is commonly used to identify if you are a healthy weight or overweight. BMI considers both height and weight.
- BMI of 25–29.9 is classed as overweight.
- BMI of 30–39.9 is classed as obese.
- BMI of 40 and above is classed as severely obese.

Key Point

For adults the BMI normal range is 18.5–24.9.

Quick Test

1. What is the healthy BMI range for an adult?
2. What is the BMI classification for a BMI of 30–39.9?
3. Since 1995 has obesity in the UK increased or decreased?

Key Words

Overweight
Obese
BMI

Energy Use, Diet, Nutrition and Hydration

You must be able to:

- Explain the role of macronutrients and micronutrients
- Explain the factors affecting optimum weight and energy balance.

Macronutrients and micronutrients include **carbohydrates, proteins** and **fats**.

Macronutrients

Carbohydrates

- Provide quick energy.
- 60% of an athlete's diet should comprise carbohydrates.
- Break down to glucose to provide fast-release energy.
- Include foods such as cereals, bread, potatoes and rice.
- Athletes will consume (carb load) carbohydrates in preparation for an event.

Protein

- Builds and repairs muscle.
- Athletes only need 15% protein in their diet.
- Athletes will consume more protein to aid recovery after competition and training.
- Power athletes such as sprinters require protein.
- Protein can be made up of meat, fish and pulses.

Water

- Helps to maintain levels of hydration.
- Prevents dehydration.
- It is important not to drink too much water or hypernatremia can be caused, which can be fatal as levels of salt and sodium can become dangerously low.

Fibre

- Is indigestible and helps avoid constipation.
- Aids healthy digestion.
- Helps maintain body weight.
- Sources include whole grain cereals, fruit and vegetables.

Micronutrients

Minerals

- Help to break down energy from food.
- Required to help intensive training and competition.
- Calcium strengthens bones.
- Iodine is needed for energy production.
- Iron prevents fatigue.

Vitamins

- Required to help the body function and aid concentration.

Key Words

Macronutrients
Micronutrients
Carbohydrates
Protein
Water
Fibre
Minerals
Vitamins

Fats

- Too much saturated fat can cause heart disease.
- Unsaturated fats are beneficial to health.
- A source of slow-release energy.
- Should be 25% of an athlete's diet.
- Source of energy for aerobic exercise.
- Sources include dairy, fish, nuts and oils.

Energy use

- The average adult male needs 2,500 Kcal/day.
- The average adult female needs 2,000 Kcal/day.

Optimum Weight

Optimum weight is where an athlete is a healthy weight that allows them to perform at their best.

Factors affecting optimum weight include sex, height, bone structure and muscle girth.

- Energy is another word for 'calories'.
- Energy balance is the balance of calories eaten compared to calories burned through physical activity.
- Energy in – this is what you eat and drink.
- Energy out – this is what you burn through physical activity.
- More physical activity, more calories burned.
- Same amount of calories burned and consumed = maintain weight.
- Consuming more calories than you burn = weight gain.
- Burning more calories than you consume = weight loss.

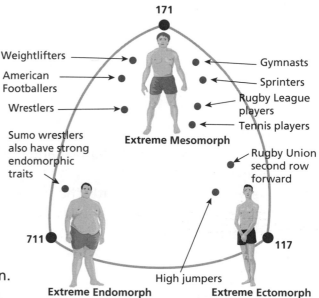

171

Weightlifters

American Footballers

Wrestlers

Gymnasts

Sprinters

Rugby League players

Tennis players

Extreme Mesomorph

Sumo wrestlers also have strong endomorphic traits

Rugby Union second row forward

711

High jumpers

117

Extreme Endomorph

Extreme Ectomorph

Hydration and Dehydration

Hydration for physical activity and sport

- During endurance activities it is important that athletes maintain hydration by drinking little and often.
- You need to be hydrated to make your body sweat and cool down.

Dehydration

- When the body's water content is reduced, it might not receive enough vitamins, salts, sugars and minerals.
- Physical performance will be reduced.
- Dehydration can be fatal.
- Blood thickening (increased viscosity) slows blood flow.
- Increase in heart rate/heart has to work harder/irregular heart rate (rhythm).
- Increase in body temperature, which can cause overheating.
- Slowing of reactions/increased reaction time/poorer decisions made.
- Muscle fatigue/cramps.

Mesomorph	Ectomorph	Endomorph
Very muscular	Very thin	Very fat
Large head	Narrow face, high forehead	Fatty upper arms
Broad shoulders	Narrow shoulders	Narrow shoulders
Strong forearms and thighs	Thin, narrow chest and abdomen	Relatively thin wrists. Fatty thighs
Narrow hips	Slim hips	Wide hips

Quick Test

1. What factors affect weight?
2. What does energy balance mean?

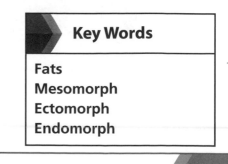

Key Words

Fats
Mesomorph
Ectomorph
Endomorph

Classification of Skills

You must be able to:

- Explain the different types of skills
- Explain the classifications of skills.

Types of Skills

Skill groupings include:

- motor skills – skills related to muscle action
- fine motor skills use intricate movements
- gross motor skills use large muscle groups.

Classification of a Range of Sports Skills using Continua

Open skills

- Sports such as basketball, football and rugby involve open skills.
- The environment is constantly changing and so movements have to be continually adapted.
- Skills are usually externally paced.

Closed skills

- These skills take place in a stable environment.
- Performer knows exactly what to do and when.
- Not affected by the environment.
- Clear beginning and end.
- Tend to be self-paced.

Basic/Simple skills

- Straightforward.
- Require little concentration.
- Limited thinking required.
- Few sub-routines.
- Limited decision-making.

Complex skills

- A complex skill involves a long attention span.
- Complicated.
- Practised in training repeatedly.
- Many sub-routines.
- Sometimes dangerous.

Low **organisation**	High organisation
• Very easy.	• Sub-routines are difficult to identify and isolate from the overall movement.
• Simple.	
• Sub-routines can be identified and easily isolated from the overall movement.	• Complex.
	• Cannot be broken down into sub-routines.

Practice Structures, Skill Classification and Relevant Practice

Each method of practice is most appropriate for particular skills.

Fixed

- Repeatedly practising the whole skill.
- Used to develop the skill.
- Best suited for closed skills.
- Example – basketball free throw.

Massed

- Continuous form of practice.
- Best suited for simple skills.
- Re-creates game situations as fatigue is caused.
- Example would be a rally in tennis.

Varied

- Variation in practice drills.
- Replicating the skill in varying scenarios.
- Best suited for open skills.
- Gets learners used to game situations.
- Example 3v2 drill in basketball.

Distributed

- Practice is divided into periods of work and rest.
- Period for mental rehearsal.
- Best suited for complex skills.
- Good for learners lacking motivation.

> **Quick Test**
>
> 1. What are the four methods of practice?
> 2. Draw the three continua.
> 3. What are motor skills?
> 4. What are fine motor skills?
> 5. What are gross motor skills?

> **Key Words**
>
> **Open skills**
> **Closed skills**
> **Simple skills**
> **Complex skills**
> **Organisation**
> **Fixed**
> **Massed**
> **Varied**
> **Distributed**

Goal Setting, SMART Targets and Information Processing

You must be able to:

- Understand the use of SMART targets
- Understand basic information processing models.

SMART

SMART targets help to:

- achieve success
- monitor improvements
- show that preparation is effective
- improve self esteem
- motivate the performer
- prevent an athlete becoming overwhelmed.

Applying the Principles of SMART Targets

Below is an example of a promising national county performer in the 400 metres.

Specific

- Goals that are set by an individual need to be specific to the sport the individual is participating in. For example an athlete attempting to run the 400 metres in under 52 seconds is clearly identifying what they are trying to achieve. Also it means that the training to help achieve this goal can be tailored to meet its demand.

Measurable

- An athlete attempting to run the 400 metres in under 52 seconds can be measured. If the athlete simply stated that they wanted to improve their time, this would not be measurable.

Achievable

- The goal needs to be a target that is achievable for the athlete otherwise it can be detrimental to an athlete's self esteem. However, the goal also needs to be difficult enough to challenge the athlete. For example, if the athlete previously mentioned is attempting to run 400 metres in under 52 seconds, this is achievable if they have run within close proximity of this time previously.

Realistic

- This means that the athlete has access to everything they need to reach the goal. For example, if the athlete cannot afford the time or financial commitment of training it is highly unlikely that they are going to achieve their goal. The goal also needs to strike a balance, making sure it is neither too challenging nor too easy.

Time-based

- A time-based deadline needs to be set alongside a goal. This is so that progress can be monitored, achievements can be celebrated and new goals can be set. Or, alternatively, if goals are not met, more realistic goals can be set and an evaluation of why the goals were not achieved could assist future improvements.

Setting and reviewing targets

- Increases motivation and resolve.
- Reinforces the importance of keeping working towards goals.
- Increases self esteem.
- Gives helpful feedback which will help identify areas for improvement.
- Can be used to set new goals.

Basic Information Processing Model

- This model can be used to understand how learning takes place and takes into consideration a feedback loop.
- Input – information sent by the body's sense organs, for example sight and sound (eyes and ears), to the brain.
- Selective attention – this is where the brain filters out any irrelevant information and focuses on what is needed.
- Decision making – this is where the participant decides what they are going to do, for example, what shot they might choose.
- Output – this is the muscles actually completing the appropriate movement after receiving messages from the brain.
- Feedback – this is where the participant thinks about whether the movement was successful and considers what to do next.

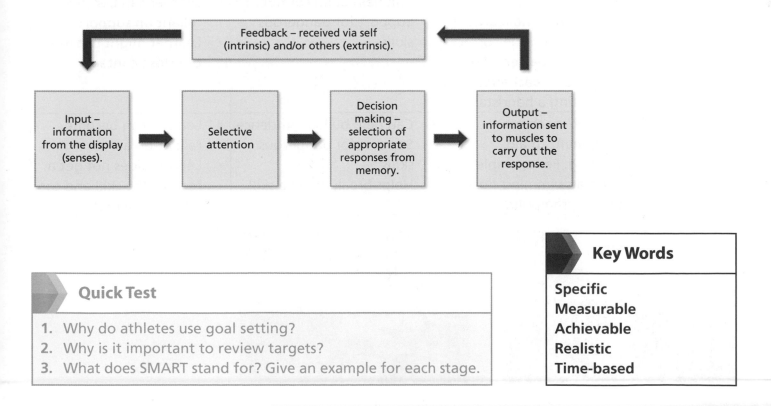

Quick Test

1. Why do athletes use goal setting?
2. Why is it important to review targets?
3. What does SMART stand for? Give an example for each stage.

Key Words

Specific
Measurable
Achievable
Realistic
Time-based

Guidance and Feedback on Performance

You must be able to:

- Explain the types of guidance for optimising performance
- Identify the strengths and weaknesses of the types of guidance
- Explain the types of feedback.

Types of Guidance

Type of Guidance	Description	Advantage(s)	Disadvantage(s)
Visual	Teacher/coach demonstrates a skill to the learner. Visual aids are used, such as video, pictures, diagrams and models. For example, a coach demonstrating the parts of a triple jump.	• Provides mental image • Shows what the skill should look like • Supports verbal instruction	• Learner can lose motivation if the skill is too difficult • Needs to be an accurate demonstration, otherwise learning will not take place and the learner will not be able to replicate
Verbal	Teacher/coach gives verbal instructions of coaching, tactics or strategies.	• Works well with visual guidance • Can give detailed feedback • Simple coaching points used for beginners	• Can be too much information for beginners • Does not work well with complex skills and can be boring
Manual	Teacher/coach physically manipulates the learner's body through the correct movement pattern. For example, a teacher/coach supporting a handstand.	• Can help build confidence • Support for dangerous skills	• Learner can become reliant on support • Learner might not like the close contact
Mechanical	Teacher/coach uses equipment to aid learning. For example, using a swimming float or a rig in trampolining.	• Can help build confidence • Support for dangerous skills • Helps break down a skill	• Learner can become reliant on aid • Learner does not get a feel for the skill and can be demotivated

Types of Feedback

Intrinsic feedback
- Tells the performer if the skill felt right.
- Self-motivating.

Extrinsic feedback
- Feedback given by teacher/coach/fans.
- Rewarding to the individual.

Concurrent feedback
- Information provided to the athlete during the performance.
- Can be used to alter performance whilst active.

Terminal feedback
- Information provided to the athlete before or after the performance.
- Can help the athlete evaluate overall performance.

Feedback and Training Data

The table below represents the fastest times run by Howard, a male 17-year-old 400-metre runner, over a seven-month period of time. From the data it is possible to analyse how the amount of time Howard spent training with a coach providing feedback affects his performance.

Month	January	February	March	April	May	June	July
Total hours spent training with a coach who provides feedback	30	40	45	50	50	60	35
Best time in seconds	52.6	52.4	52.2	51.9	51.9	51.6	52.1

Training Data

From the data provided:
- the fastest time run was in June and the slowest in January
- the most amount of time spent with a coach providing feedback was in June and the least in January
- when Howard spends the most amount of time with a coach providing feedback he has the best results and runs the fastest times. Whereas the least amount of time spent results in the slowest times.

Key Points

Guidance is advice or information given to help an individual or team to improve. There are four main types of guidance used to improve sport and physical activity; visual, verbal, manual and mechanical.

Review: to assess and evaluate and then apply this to physical activity and sport. An example would be to assess performance in a recent competition and identify what needs to be done to improve.

Key Words

Visual
Verbal
Manual
Mechanical
Intrinsic
Extrinsic
Concurrent
Terminal

Quick Test

1. What are the four types of guidance?
2. Identify the four types of feedback.
3. What are the advantages and disadvantages of each type of guidance?

Mental Preparation, Arousal and Personality

You must be able to:

- Explain the reasons for a psychological warm-up
- Explain how mental rehearsal can affect performance
- Explain how arousal and personality can affect performance.

Psychological Preparation

Psychological warm-up

- Helps an athlete get into a positive mindset.
- Helps an athlete focus and relax.

Methods used to Prepare Mentally

- Positive self-talk: using motivational and encouraging words, for example 'I can' or 'I will'.
- Imagery: where a performer visualises the performance.
- Performance evaluation: identifies strengths and areas for improvement.
- Relaxation sessions: can help a performer manage levels of stress.

The Benefits of Mental Rehearsal

- Helps an individual to control emotions/feelings/arousal.
- Assists an individual in making the correct decisions.
- Can make sure an individual is playing fairly.
- Enables an individual to reduce stress levels and maintain focus.
- The individual can then make more logical/calmer decisions and play fairer/show sportsmanship.
- Allows a performer to cope better with stress/anxiety/focus.
- Enables an individual to correctly use selective attention.
- Allows the performer to react more quickly.
- Can develop confidence and/or positive thoughts.

Arousal

As a sports performer it is important to be at the correct levels of arousal. Being under-aroused or over-aroused can cause performance issues.

Inverted-U theory

- This graph is the shape of an inverted-U.
- The y-axis represents performance level – low to high.
- The x-axis represents arousal level – low to high.
- The graph has an optimal zone, where the best performance results occur, where the performer is not under- or over-aroused.

> **Key Point**
>
> Psychological warm-up is how an individual or team will mentally prepare themselves for competition or training.

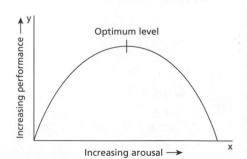

- When under-aroused, performance level is low.
- Over-arousal also causes low performance levels.
- Optimal arousal levels vary according to the skill.
- For example a tackle in rugby will need a high arousal level, whereas a snooker shot will possibly need lower arousal.

Arousal can be controlled using stress management techniques, which include:
- deep breathing
- mental rehearsal/visualisation/use of imagery
- positive self-talk.

Characteristics of Personality Types

Introverts:
- are shy/quiet/thoughtful
- enjoy being on their own
- tend to play individual sports where concentration/precision (fine skills) are required, with low arousal.

Extroverts:
- enjoy interaction with others/are sociable/aroused by others
- are enthusiastic/talkative
- are prone to boredom when isolated/by themselves
- tend to play team sports where there is a fast pace, concentration may be low, and gross skills are used.

Motivation
- Intrinsic: is from within, e.g. pride, self-satisfaction, personal achievement.
- Extrinsic: is from another source, e.g. to gain certificates, win trophies, be awarded medals, intangible sources, etc.

> **Key Point**
>
> Mental preparation can often make the difference between success and failure in elite athletes and it is increasingly becoming an area of investigation by sport scientists.

> **Key Point**
>
> Personality: the sum of characteristics that make a person unique.
>
> Motivation: the direction and intensity of an individual's effort.
>
> Arousal: the psychological state of alertness that prepares the body for action.

> **Quick Test**
>
> 1. Why do athletes undertake mental preparation?
> 2. Define mental rehearsal.
> 3. Mental rehearsal is a useful method to help achieve the correct levels of motivation. True or False?

> **Key Words**
>
> Preparation
> Mental rehearsal

Practice Questions

Physical, Emotional and Social Health, Fitness and Well-being

1 Which of the following is the best method to improve physical health?

Tick (✓) one answer.

a) Losing weight ( )

b) Controlling emotions ( )

c) Making friends ( )

d) Learning to adapt to change ( ) [1]

2 Which of the following is an outcome of having good emotional health?

Tick (✓) one answer.

a) Losing weight ( )

b) Able to control emotions ( )

c) Improved flexibility ( )

d) Improved cardio-vascular fitness ( ) [1]

Total Marks _____ / 2

The Consequences of a Sedentary Lifestyle

1 Identify the long-term health risks of being overweight/obese.

_____

_____

_____

_____

_____

_____ [3]

Total Marks _____ / 3

Energy Use, Diet, Nutrition and Hydration

1 Explain the role of macronutrients in maintaining a healthy lifestyle and maximising optimal performance.

_____

_____

_____

_____

_____

_____ [3]

2 Explain the role of micronutrients in maintaining a healthy lifestyle and maximising optimal performance.

_____

_____

_____

_____

_____

_____ [3]

3 Explain the effect that dehydration can have on sports performers.

_____

_____

_____ [3]

Total Marks _____ / 9

Classification of Skills

 1 Explain different aspects of skills.

a) Explain what is meant by an open skill and a closed skill. Include examples in your answer.

_____

_____

_____

_____

_____

_____

_____

_____ [4]

b) Explain what is meant by a basic (simple) skill and a complex skill. Include examples in your answer.

_____

_____

_____

_____

_____

_____

_____ [4]

c) Explain what is meant by a low organisation skill and a high organisation skill. Include examples in your answer.

_____

_____

_____

_____

_____

_____

_____

_____ [4]

Total Marks _____ / 12

Goal Setting, SMART Targets and Information Processing

1 Explain two reasons why Evie-Marie might set and review her targets when training for her county athletics competitions.

_____

_____

_____

_____ [2]

Total Marks _____ / 2

Practice Questions

Guidance and Feedback on Performance

1 Analyse the following types of guidance.

a) Visual:

_____

_____

_____

_____

_____ [3]

b) Verbal:

_____

_____

_____

_____

_____ [3]

c) Mechanical:

_____

_____

_____

_____

_____

_____ [3]

2 Describe manual guidance and how it can optimise performance.

_____

_____

_____

_____

_____

_____ [3]

Total Marks _____ / 12

Mental Preparation, Arousal and Personality

1 What is mental rehearsal used for?

Tick (✓) one answer.

a) Improving flexibility ( )

b) Developing coordination ( )

c) Making friends ( )

d) Being able to control emotions and mental state ( ) [1]

Total Marks _____ / 1

Lever Systems

1 Match the key term with the correct description.

Fulcrum	The body's weight or an external object.
Effort	The point of movement or pivot, generally at the centre of a joint.
Load	The muscular force applied.

[3]

2 Match the key term with the correct description.

First class	Effort in the middle
Second class	Resistance in the middle
Third class	Fulcrum in the middle

[3]

3 Identify two advantages and two disadvantages of first class levers.

Advantages:

_____

_____

_____

_____ [2]

Disadvantages:

_____

_____

_____

_____ [2]

Total Marks _____ / 10

Planes and Axes of Movement

1 Match the key term with the correct description.

Sagittal plane	Passes from side to side at right angles to the sagittal plane, which separates the body into front and back sections.
Frontal plane	A vertical plane, which passes from front to rear, separating the body into right and left parts.
Transverse plane	A horizontal plane that separates the body into upper and lower parts.

[3]

2 Match the key term with the correct description.

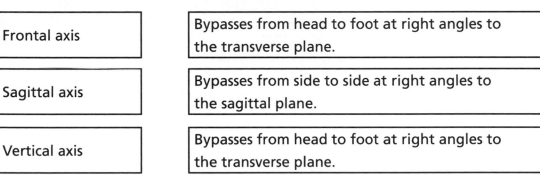

Frontal axis	Bypasses from head to foot at right angles to the transverse plane.
Sagittal axis	Bypasses from side to side at right angles to the sagittal plane.
Vertical axis	Bypasses from head to foot at right angles to the transverse plane.

[3]

Total Marks _____ / 6

The Relationship between Health and Fitness

1 Identify five positives of improving an individual's fitness.

_____

_____

_____

_____

_____

_____

_____

_____

_____

_____ [5]

2 Identify three potential negatives of undertaking fitness training.

_____

_____

_____

_____

_____

_____ [3]

Total Marks _____ / 8

Components of Fitness Data Interpretation

Harvard step test

Measures cardio-vascular fitness (aerobic endurance).

Normative data, 16-year-old athlete

Gender	Excellent	Above Average	Average	Below Average	Poor
Male	>90	80–90	65–79	55–64	<55
Female	>86	76–86	61–75	50–60	<50

Using the table above, correctly identify the level of fitness for the following individuals.

Tick (✓) one answer for each question.

1 Emily, who is a 16-year-old female, has a score of 88.

a) excellent

b) average

c) below average

d) poor [1]

2 Heidi, who is a 16-year-old female, has a score of 48.

a) excellent

b) average

c) below average

d) poor [1]

3 Herbert, who is a 16-year-old male, has a score of 66.

a) excellent

b) average

c) below average

d) poor [1]

Total Marks _____ / 3

The Principles of Training

1 Explain the principle of specificity and give an example.

_____

_____

_____

_____

_____

_____

_____

_____

_____ [4]

2 Explain the dangers of overtraining.

_____

_____

_____

_____

_____

_____ [3]

3 Explain how an athlete can improve their aerobic threshold.

_____

_____

_____

_____

_____ [3]

4 Explain how an athlete can improve their anaerobic threshold.

_____

_____

_____

_____

_____

_____

_____

_____

_____

_____ [3]

Total Marks _____ / 13

The Long-term Effects of Exercise

1 Identify the effects of undertaking long-term training.

_____

_____

_____

_____

_____ [5]

Review Questions

2 Explain the benefits to the musculo-skeletal system of undertaking long-term training.

_____

_____

_____

_____

_____

_____

_____

_____

_____

_____ [5]

3 Explain the benefits to the cardio-respiratory system of undertaking long-term training.

_____

_____

_____

_____

_____

_____

_____

_____

_____

_____

_____

_____ [6]

Total Marks _____ / 16

How to Optimise Training and Prevent Injury

1 What is a Pre-Activity Readiness Questionnaire (PARQ)? Explain its use.

_____

_____

_____

_____

_____

_____ [3]

2 Describe the following injuries:

Dislocation:

_____

_____ [1]

Sprain:

_____

_____ [1]

Torn cartilage:

_____

_____ [1]

3 Name five different types of performance-enhancing drugs.

_____

_____

_____

_____

_____ [5]

Total Marks _____ / 11

Review Questions

Effective Use of Warm-up and Cool Down

1 Identify the four stages of a warm-up.

_____

_____

_____

_____

_____

_____

_____

_____ [4]

2 Explain the aims of a cool down.

_____

_____

_____

_____

_____

_____ [3]

Total Marks _____ / 7

Use of Data

1 The table below shows normative data for the 12-minute Cooper run test.

Age	Excellent	Above average	Average	Below average	Poor
Males 13–14	>2700 m	2400–2700 m	2200–2399 m	2100–2199 m	<2100 m
Females 13–14	>2000 m	1900–2000 m	1600–1899 m	1500–1599 m	<1500 m
Males 15–16	>2800 m	2500–2800 m	2300–2499 m	2200–2299 m	<2200 m
Females 15–16	>2100 m	2000–2100 m	1700–1999 m	1600–1699 m	<1600 m
Males 17–19	>3000 m	2700–3000 m	2500–2699 m	2300–2499 m	<2300 m
Females 17–19	>2300 m	2100–2300 m	1800-2099 m	1700–1799 m	<1700 m

Identify the level of fitness of each participant.

a) Emily, female, age 13 – 2892 metres

_____ [1]

b) Sunil, male, age 18 – 2224 metres

_____ [1]

c) Holly, female, age 19 – 1801 metres

_____ [1]

2 The data table below can be used to compare normative results for 16–19 year-olds for the grip dynamometer test.

Gender	Excellent	Good	Average	Fair	Poor
Male	>56	51–56	45–50	39–44	<39
Female	>36	31–36	25–30	19–24	<19

Identify the level of fitness of each participant.

a) Callum, male – 54

_____ [1]

b) Amal, female – 38

_____ [1]

3 The data table below can be used to compare normative results for a 30-m sprint test. The test measures speed.

Gender	Excellent	Above average	Average	Below average	Poor
Male	<4	4.0–4.2	4.3–4.4	4.5–4.6	>4.6
Female	<4.5	4.5–4.6	4.7–4.8	4.9–5.0	>5

Identify the level of fitness of each participant.

a) Kanu, female – 5.6 seconds

_____ [1]

b) Rory, male – 4.55 seconds

_____ [1]

4 The vertical jump test identifies power. Using the data table, identify the level of fitness of Ade, Bradley and Jessica in comparison to world-class athletes.

% Rank	Females	Males
91–100	76.20–81.30 cm	86.35–91.45 cm
81–90	71.11–76.19 cm	81.30–86.34 cm
71–80	66.05–71.10 cm	76.20–81.29 cm
61–70	60.95–66.04 cm	71.10–76.19 cm
51–60	55.90–60.94 cm	66.05–71.09 cm
41–50	50.80–55.89 cm	60.95–66.04 cm
31–40	45.71–50.79 cm	55.90–60.94 cm
21–30	40.65–45.70 cm	50.80–55.89 cm
11–20	35.55–40.64 cm	45.70–50.79 cm
1–10	30.50–35.54 cm	40.65–45.69 cm

Identify the percentage rank of each participant.

a) Ade, male – 44 cm

_____ [1]

b) Bradley, male – 68 cm

_____ [1]

c) Jessica, female – 77 cm

_____ [1]

5 The data table below can be used to compare normative results for a one minute sit-up test.

Normative data

Male 18–25		Female 18–25	
Excellent	>49	Excellent	>43
Good	44–49	Good	37–43
Above average	39–43	Above average	33–36
Average	35–38	Average	29–32
Below average	31–34	Below average	25–28
Poor	25–30	Poor	18–24
Very poor	<24	Very poor	<18

Identify the level of fitness of each participant (muscular endurance).

a) Dominic, male – 41 _____ [1]

b) Laura, female – 44 _____ [1]

6 The data table below can be used to compare normative results for a one minute press-up test.

Normative data

Male 18–25		Female 18–25	
Excellent	>56	Excellent	>35
Good	47–56	Good	27–35
Above average	35–46	Above average	21–26
Average	19–34	Average	11–20
Below average	11–18	Below average	6–10
Poor	4–10	Poor	2–5
Very poor	<4	Very poor	<2

Identify the level of fitness of each participant (muscular endurance).

a) Paul, male – 6 _____ [1]

b) Beverly, female – 29 _____ [1]

c) Lucy, female – 58 _____ [1]

Total Marks _____ / 15

Engagement Patterns of Different Social Groups in Physical Activity and Sport 1

You must be able to:

- Explain the participation rates that affect different social groups
- Interpret and analyse graphical data on trends in participation.

Participation Rates in Physical Activity and Sport: Gender and Age

Gender

- Women do less sport than men.
- There are fewer opportunities for women to engage in sport.
- Some women fear being judged.
- Some women lack the confidence to take part.
- Opportunities for women in sport are increasing, but are still low in some areas.
- Some religious values do not support women taking part in sport.

Age

- Physically demanding sports are usually chosen by younger people, for example rugby, football and netball.
- Older people often participate in sports that are less physically demanding and are not high impact, for example swimming and walking.
- Younger people often cite lack of time for participation.
- Older people often cite ill health as a reason not to participate in sport.
- Lack of age-specific groups/clubs can affect participation.
- The introduction of veterans' walking football has helped to increase participation.

Interpretation and Analysis of Graphical Data: trends in participation

Active People Survey 2014

Gender

- Men (60.8%) take part in sport.
- Women (46.0%) take part in sport.
- The top five sports for both men and women include swimming, cycling and health and fitness.
- Women are more likely than men to do aerobics and go running, while men are more likely to play football or snooker.

> **Key Point**
>
> Target groups are disadvantaged communities that have been identified by various sporting organisations as being underrepresented in sport and physical activity. They include women, disabled people, old people and the unemployed.

> **Key Point**
>
> There are many specific groups of society that have lower participation rates, you specifically need to know the five main groups.

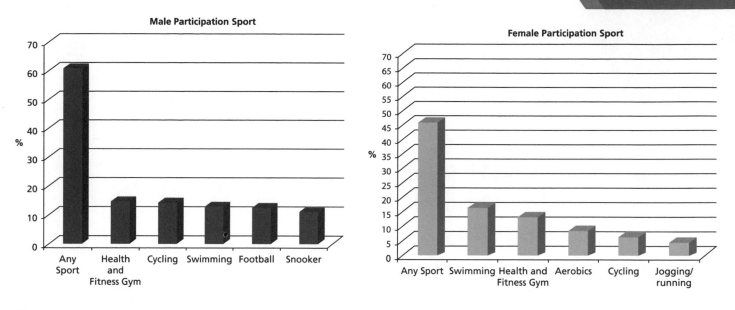

Age

- 65–74 year-olds do more exercise than other age groups, but most of that exercise is low intensity walking.
- Less than a quarter of young people participate in sport (16–24).
- Less than a third of all people meet the government recommended weekly guidelines for physical exercise.

Frequency of participation in physical activity, by age

Frequency					
	Age 16–24	Age 25–44	Age 45–64	Age 65–74	Age 75+
Once or twice a month	18%	19.5%	18.9%	18.1%	19.5%
Once a week	21.6%	20.2%	20.1%	21.7%	31.1%
Two or three times a week	24.6%	29.7%	28.5%	32.6%	27.9%
More than four times a week	17.1%	16.9%	16.5%	12.5%	–

Quick Test

1. Do more males or females participate in sport and physical activity?
2. What age group usually participates in vigorous physical activity the most?
3. State three reasons why females might not participate in sport and physical activity.

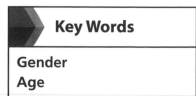

Key Words

Gender
Age

Engagement Patterns of Different Social Groups in Physical Activity and Sport 2

You must be able to:

- Explain the participation rates that affect different social groups
- Interpret and analyse graphical data on trends in participation.

Participation Rates in Physical Activity and Sport: Socio-economic Group, Ethnicity and Disability

Socio-economic group

- Levels of disposable income and social status can affect participation.
- All sports are available if they can be afforded.
- Some people cannot afford sports equipment.
- Some people cannot afford to travel to play sport.
- Some people cannot get to/afford sports facilities.
- Leisure providers often have a reduction in entry fees for people who are currently unemployed or are over the age of 60.

Ethnicity

- Participation by ethnic minorities in some instances is lower than other groups.
- Racist behaviour can prevent individuals from taking part in sport.
- Lack of sufficient specific classes for ethnic minorities.
- Lack of role models.
- Participation is increasing for ethnic minorities in sport.

Disability

- A limited range of activities is sometimes an issue.
- The number of disabled people who take part in sport has risen significantly, but barriers remain.
- Funding can be an issue.
- Lack of specialist coaches/clubs/classes can affect attendance.
- Lack of specialist facilities can affect attendance.
- Lack of specialist equipment can affect attendance.

Interpretation and Analysis of Graphical Data: trends in participation

Active People Survey 2014

Socio-economic group

- Highest levels of participation are amongst individuals with the highest income.

- People with an income of under £10,000 have the lowest levels of participation in sport.
- Individuals with the lowest income sometimes have access to free classes to help maintain physical activity.

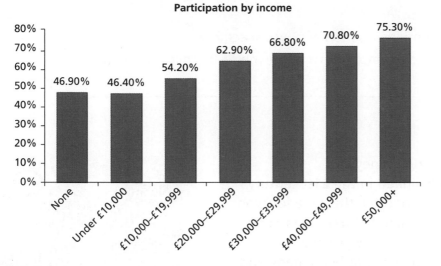

Participation by income

Ethnicity

- For ethnic minority groups overall the participation rate in sport is 40% compared with a national average of 46%.
- The gap between men's and women's participation in sport is greater amongst some ethnic minority groups than it is in the population as a whole.

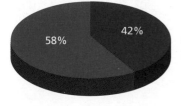

Ethnic Minorities Participation

42%
58%
- Participate in physical activity
- Do not participate in physical activity

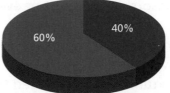

National Average Participation

40%
60%
- Participate in physical activity
- Do not participate in physical activity

Disability

- Participation for adults with disabilities is rising.
- However, the picture varies depending on the type of disability. People with sensory impairments have a particularly low participation rate, at just 13.4%.

Who plays sport?
The number of adults with a limiting disability or illness who participate once a week

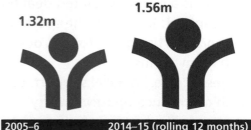

1.32m
1.56m

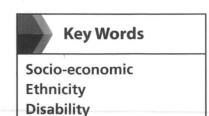

2005–6   2014–15 (rolling 12 months)

Source: Active People Survey 8Q3-9Q2 (Sport England, 2014–15)

Quick Test

1. Name the five groups of people whose participation in sport is sometimes lowest.
2. Give three reasons why people in a lower socio-economic group might not be able to participate in sport.
3. Give three reasons why ethnicity might affect participation in sport.

Commercialisation of Physical Activity and Sport

You must be able to:
- Explain the commercialisation of physical activity
- Explain the role of sponsorship and the media in physical activity.

Commercialism

Commercialism is the emphasis on making money.
- Commercialism and sport are closely linked in the 21st century.
- Commercialism is a major feature of sport; often there is a focus on maximising profit at the expense of the values of traditional sport.
- However, there are many examples of how sports have developed thanks to commercialism, money has been made and sales increased.
- Brings new audiences and publicity to sports.
- Participation in some sports has increased.
- **Sponsorship** has increased income in sport/for performers.
- **Media** companies pay huge sums of money for television rights and to be linked with athletes/teams.
- Media coverage of sport is extensive.
- It is easier to get sponsorship if a sport or event obtains media interest.
- High-profile events receive more sponsorship than those with little or no media coverage.
- Dates and times of fixtures can be changed to suit audiences.

Sponsorship and Sport

Sponsorship is a business-related deal that provides financial and material support. In return, the sport/performer or team acts as a promotion/advertising site for a product or service. Sponsorship comes in many forms:
- businesses give financial support, equipment or expertise, which can reduce financial worry
- teams or individuals receive support in return for promoting a company logo which can include free kit, clothing and equipment
- company image is enriched
- can increase sales
- most clubs have sponsors
- most competitions/stadia now have sponsors, which can be seen as negative
- if a performer/team behaves badly it can be associated with the sponsor
- players/teams can be tied to wearing specific clothing/kit.

Key Point

The close link between sport and business is a modern phenomenon – until recently participants in sport were all amateur and played for the love of the game, e.g. Rugby Union did not turn professional until 1995. Modern sport is often run in a similar way to a business with a focus on making money.

Media

Media is communication through both written and electronic forms. Media outlets will sometimes exaggerate and dramatise a story to increase their sales, at the cost of impartial journalism – focusing on what they think a reader will want to read, rather than reporting the events that actually happen. Local media is often written with an emphasis on appealing to local fans.

Sport and the Media

The pros and cons of media coverage

	Pros	Cons
Media involvement	• Increased publicity • Increased sales/revenue	• Events can be exaggerated to increase interest and damage the reputation of the sport • Values of the sport can be lost
Sport	• Increased revenue • Attendance may rise as people want to see the 'stars' • Easier to attract sponsorship • Attracts new audience	• Dates/times of fixtures changed • Attendance may drop • Some sports get no 'air time' • Changing of rules
Player/performer	• Increased exposure • Free clothing and equipment • Reduces financial worries • Professional support	• Player/performer tied to wearing specific clothing/kit • Commercial sponsor appearances can affect performance and training
Spectator/fans	• Better-informed supporters • Increased awareness of the sport • Lots of coverage • Viewed globally	• Changing of fixture times and dates • Seasons for a sport changing to a different time of year, e.g. traditional season being altered to cater for a television audience

Interpretation and Analysis of Graphical Data: commercialisation

• In 1992–97 – when the Premier League was formed the TV rights were sold for £191 million.
• In 2016–19 – the TV rights for the Premier League were sold for £5.1 billion.
• Over the last 20 years many sports have become increasingly commercial, with huge sums of money coming into sport.

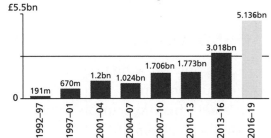

Rise of Premier League TV income

£5.5bn

5.136bn
3.018bn
1.706bn 1.773bn
1.2bn 1.024bn
670m
191m

1992–97
1997–01
2001–04
2004–07
2007–10
2010–13
2013–16
2016–19

Quick Test

1. Define media.
2. Define commercialisation.
3. Define sponsorship.
4. Has the income for TV rights in football risen for every deal?

Key Words

Commercialism
Sponsorship
Media

Ethical and Socio-cultural Issues in Physical Activity and Sport

You must be able to:

- Explain different types of behaviour
- Using graphical data, identify and analyse trends in ethical and socio-cultural issues.

Different Types of Sporting Behaviour

Behaviours

- **Sportsmanship**: qualities of fairness, following the rules, being gracious in defeat or victory. For example, England cricketer Andrew Flintoff, rather than celebrating winning a crucial match levelling the series, chose to commiserate with and support his defeated opponent.
- **Gamesmanship**: bending the rules/laws of a sport without actually breaking them.
- **Deviance**: behaviour that goes against the moral values or laws of the sport. For example, taking drugs or feigning injury.

The Advantages of Sportsmanship

- Having elite performers demonstrating high levels of sportsmanship is good for the sport because it will increase the likelihood of sportsmanship at the foundation stages.
- Professional sports people are role models for young people and positive behaviour can lead to more people taking part in a particular sport.
- High-profile sports stars get significant amounts of media coverage, therefore it is important for performers to behave appropriately.

Reasons for Deviance in Elite Sport

- Focus only on winning.
- Pressure to win.
- Pressure from spectators to win.
- Media involvement.
- Emotional intensity of fixtures.
- Fatigue.
- Frustration.
- Poor officiating.
- Pressure to perform.
- Pressure to win prize money.

The Consequences of Deviance in Elite Sport

- Fines for clubs or individuals.
- Bans for clubs or individuals.
- Negative image for participant(s).
- Negative image of the sport.
- Sponsors or commercial partners withdraw.
- Negative media portrayal.
- Loss of income to club/individual.

Number of Cyclists Caught Taking Drugs in International Competition

- The table displays the number of international cyclists caught using performance-enhancing drugs between 2000 and 2010.
- The actual number is assumed by many to be much higher, there have been many high-profile cyclists, including Lance Armstrong, who were not caught but have since admitted doping in this period.
- In 2000, there were six cases of doping in cycling worldwide, which was the lowest number.
- The peak years were 2006 and 2007, where 76 cyclists were caught in two years.
- The data possibly suggests that testing is becoming more rigorous and athletes are being caught more regularly.
- Alternatively, fewer athletes are choosing to use performance-enhancing drugs or more athletes are avoiding being caught.

> ### Key Point
>
> Professional sport is full of deviance – professionals will do almost anything they can to win. For example, it is not uncommon for a football player to dive or pretend to be injured to gain an advantage. Whereas in amateur sport participants will often focus more on playing fairly and demonstrating sportsmanship.

Year	2000	2001	2002	2003	2004	2005	2006	2007	2008	2009	2010
Number of Cyclists Caught Doping	6	9	14	7	28	20	44	32	28	15	24

Quick Test

1. Define and give an example of sportsmanship.
2. Define and give an example of gamesmanship.
3. Define and give an example of deviance in sports.

Key Words

Sportsmanship
Gamesmanship
Deviance

Contemporary Sport

You must be able to:

- Explain the reasons for deviance in sport
- Explain the influence of spectators and television on performers
- Understand the advantages and disadvantages of using PEDs for the performer.

Violence

Violence in sport is unfortunately a regular occurrence. There are many reasons for this, just some of which include:

- frustration due to the result of the game/match/race
- poor officiating
- provocation
- religion/tradition
- cheating
- the importance of the fixture
- late tackles in football
- high tackles in rugby
- aggressive bowling in cricket
- body shots in tennis
- obstructing an opponent in basketball
- high stick in hockey.

Hooliganism

Bad behaviour by spectators also takes place. There are many reasons for this and various strategies have been created to combat spectator violence.

Reasons for hooliganism	Strategies employed to combat hooliganism
Rivalries/religion	Early kick-offs
Hype	All-seater stadia
Fuelled by alcohol/drugs	Segregation of fans
Gang culture	Improved security
Frustration	Alcohol restrictions
Display of masculinity	Travel restrictions/banning orders

Etiquette

- **Etiquette:** the correct ways to behave while competing in sport.
- **Direct aggression:** where physical contact is deliberately made, for example punching in boxing or tackling in rugby.
- **Indirect aggression:** where players hit a ball to 'beat' their opponents, for example cricket to beat a fielder.

The Influence of Spectators at Sporting Events

Positives	Negatives
Creation of atmosphere	Negative effect on performance as a result of increased pressure
Home-field advantage	Potential for crowd trouble/hooliganism
Can inspire people to take part	Safety costs/concerns
	Negative effect on participation numbers amongst younger people

The Influence of Television on Sport

Positives	Negatives
• Cash: media companies pay to be allowed to show live sporting fixtures. This money can be put back into the sport.	• With fixtures being televised, live spectators might choose not to attend games, which negatively affects attendances.
• Inspirational role models can be generated from being on television, which can lead to an increase in participation.	• Only mainstream sports are shown on television, leaving some sports with very limited or no coverage at all.
• Television enables performers to learn new skills.	• Disruption caused by change of date and time of fixtures.

Advantages and Disadvantages of Using PEDs for the Performer

Unfortunately, for some elite sports people, taking performance enhancing drugs has many advantages, even though it is against the rules. These include:
- increased chances of success
- fame
- wealth
- makes it a level playing field as many others possibly take PEDs too.

However, disadvantages include:
- cheating/immoral
- associated health risks
- fines
- bans
- reputational damage
- loss of sponsorship.

> ### Quick Test
>
> 1. Identify three reasons for violence in sport.
> 2. Identify three reasons why any athlete might choose to use performance-enhancing drugs.
> 3. Explain three ways in which television has positively impacted on sport.

Key Words

Etiquette
Hooliganism

Use of Data

You must be able to:

- Understand how data is collected
- Understand how to present data and interpret results.

How to Collect Data

Data can be collected in various different ways, including:

- face to face, where you can discuss results or information with a client
- telephone conversations
- using post, where individuals reply to a predetermined request for information
- using the internet, where information can be used, shared, interpreted and recorded quickly and efficiently.

Forms of Data Collection

Questionnaires are often used to collect data and information. A well-structured questionnaire could have simple answers with just a couple of responses or alternatively tick-boxes. Or questionnaires can require short written responses.

It is often necessary to gather data and information about an individual's fitness level, which can be done in many different ways. Whichever method is selected, it is essential that it does not affect the results and their reliability. There are several methods that can be used to generate data, which can then be analysed. These methods include:

- the use of video to allow performance analysis and visual evidence
- completing an observation schedule, which is quick and simple to use and can identify strengths and weaknesses
- the use of heart rate monitors to record performers'/ participants' training zones, which can then be analysed
- self-reflection, which can be used by performers/participants to identify their thoughts and feelings about a performance.

> **Key Point**
>
> The simplest way to collect data is to use a tally chart, but you will need to be able to interpret other methods.

Using standardised fitness tests is a good way to collect data about a performer or participants. It is essential that these tests are completed following the format in which they have been developed to make them valid and reliable.

There are many more sophisticated data collection techniques, being invented and utilised. Modern techniques provide the opportunity to gather real time performance data.

Presenting Data

Bar charts are used to compare two or more values, with the height of each bar showing the frequency of the outcome. The vertical bar is usually labelled frequency; the horizontal varies depending on what is being measured.

Line graphs can be used to show trends in data over a specific period of time. The respondent's data is plotted as a series of points, which are then joined with straight lines.

Pie charts display data through proportioning into segments, which is in correlation to the data recorded. This is usually done by working out the fraction of the total that the sector represents, then converting this to an angle, which is drawn as a sector in the chart. Many people now draw pie charts using computer software.

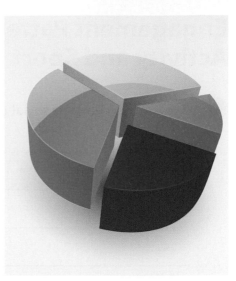

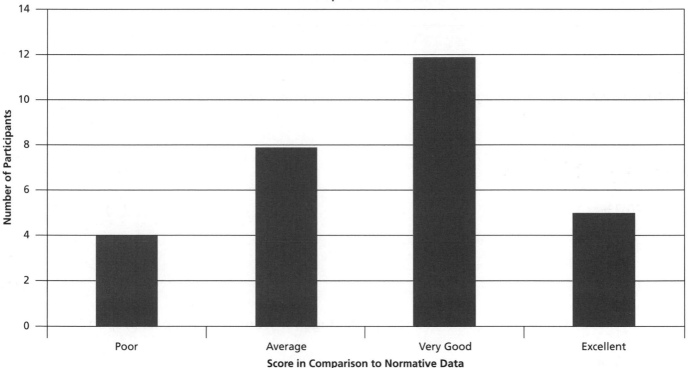

Class Cooper Run Fitness Results

Quick Test

1. Name four different ways to collect data.
2. Identify three methods to present data.

Key Words

Data
Presenting data

Engagement Patterns of Different Social Groups in Physical Activity and Sport

1 Explain why various social groups have lower participation rates in sport and physical activity.

_____

_____

_____

_____

_____

_____

_____ [3]

2 Which one of the following is the correct percentage for men taking part in sport?

Tick (✓) one answer.

a) 60.8%   ( )

b) 70.2%   ( )

c) 46.0%   ( )

d) 15.5%   ( )   [1]

3 Which one of the following is the correct percentage for women taking part in sport?

Tick (✓) one answer.

a) 60.8%   ( )

b) 70.2%   ( )

c) 46.0%   ( )

d) 15.5%   ( )   [1]

> **Total Marks** _____ / 5

Commercialisation of Physical Activity and Sport

1 Analyse the effects of commercialism in sport.

_____

_____

_____

_____

_____

_____

_____ [3]

2 Commercialism is:

a) the emphasis on making money. ☐

b) the emphasis on increasing participation. ☐

c) improving health and fitness. ☐

d) developing safe sport. ☐ [1]

3 Sponsorship is:

a) a deal that provides financial support in return for promotion/advertising. ☐

b) the emphasis on increasing participation. ☐

c) selling of sporting merchandise and equipment. ☐

d) the performer/team being supported by a governing body. ☐ [1]

Total Marks _____ / 5

Ethical and Socio-cultural Issues in Physical Activity and Sport

1 Explain the following terms:

Sportsmanship:

_____

_____

_____ [1]

Gamesmanship:

_____

_____

_____ [1]

Deviance:

_____

_____

_____ [1]

Total Marks _____ / 3

Contemporary Sport

1 Spectators can influence sporting events or matches in both positive and negative ways.

   a) Explain two positives.

   _____

   _____ [2]

   b) Explain two negatives.

   _____

   _____ [2]

2 There are many different strategies to prevent crowd trouble at spectator events. Explain three different crowd control strategies.

_____

_____

_____ [3]

Use of Data

1 What is quantitative research?

_____

_____ [1]

2 What is qualitative research?

_____

_____ [1]

Total Marks _____ / 9

Physical, Emotional and Social Health, Fitness and Well-being

1 Fill in the gaps for the definition of health.

Health is a s_____ of whole p_____, m_____ and s_____ well-being and with the absence of disease, illness or injury. [1]

2 Physical health is made up of various factors. Tick (✓) the best description of physical health. [1]

a) Your own unique physiological profile, the environment you live in, eating a healthy diet, undertaking regular exercise and being able to access necessary healthcare. ☐

b) How you deal with disappointing results or outcomes. Being prepared to accept challenges. Fitting into different social situations and getting on well with different types of people. ☐

c) Being able to devote time to leisure activities, free from the constraints of work and other commitments. Having enough disposable income to pay for activities when you wish. ☐

3 Tick (✓) the best description of emotional health. [1]

a) Distinct natural make-up, the location you live in, living a sensible lifestyle, being able to receive necessary medical care. ☐

b) The ability to come back from defeat or disappointment. The will to take on difficult situations, make new friends and be comfortable in different social situations. ☐

c) Sport and physical activity is given enough time in your schedule and you have sufficient money to take part in any sport whenever you want. You are also able to plan and encourage other individuals to participate in sport. ☐

4 Tick (✓) the best description of social health. [1]

a) Run, swim or cycle a long distance without getting out of breath. The ability to train in the multi-gym and to not ache the next day. ☐

b) Have positive relationships with other people and to fit into varying social situations. Whilst within different social situations behave suitably and communicate freely with all. ☐

c) Having enough time and money to participate in sport and physical activity whenever you wish. The ability to plan and motivate other people to take part in sport. Not smoking, drinking or taking drugs, and undertaking regular cardio-vascular exercise. ☐

5 Match each training principle to the correct description. One has been done for you. [5]

Specificity	Variation is needed in training programmes to prevent boredom.
Progression	It is essential to allow time to recover from periods of training or adaptations will not occur.
Overload	Any adaptation will be lost if you take a break in training.
Reversibility	Steadily increase the intensity of activity and keep overloading; doing so too quickly can lead to problems.
Rest (recovery)	Gains are only made in fitness when training is more demanding than previously undertaken.
Tedium	Training must be coordinated to the requirements of the activity and to the individual.

6 When developing a fitness programme, the following FITT principle should be applied. Match each training principle to the correct description. One has been done for you. [3]

Frequency	The amount of effort you put into your training. Training at great demand will benefit the body.
Intensity	The amount of times a week training is undertaken. Undertaking more days of training will result in improvements.
Time	Adapting the method used can increase the level of overload.
Type	Duration of training sessions; this can be increased to overload the body.

7 Explain the various methods that can be used to evaluate the effectiveness of an individual's training.

_____

_____

_____

_____

_____

_____ [3]

Total Marks _____ / 15

The Consequences of a Sedentary Lifestyle

1 Diet is one of the most significant factors that affects physical fitness. Explain one positive and one negative impact of this lifestyle choice.

_____

_____

_____

_____ [2]

2 Explain the positive and negative implications of improving fitness.

Positive:

_____

_____

_____

_____ [2]

Negative:

_____

_____

_____

_____ [2]

3 There are consequences of having a sedentary lifestyle or an active lifestyle. (Circle) the correct answers below.

a) Depression is less likely to occur if you don't have a sedentary lifestyle.

        True   False   [1]

b) Coronary heart disease is more likely to occur if you do not undertake any exercise.

        True   False   [1]

c) Low blood pressure is less likely to occur if you eat a balanced diet.

        True   False   [1]

d) Diabetes is more likely to occur if you are overweight.

        True   False   [1]

e) There is an increased risk of osteoporosis if you do not participate in physical activity.

        True   False   [1]

f) You will suffer a loss of muscle if you do not participate in physical activity.

        True   False   [1]

g) Poor posture is less likely to occur if you undertake regular physical activity.

        True   False   [1]

h) Poor physical fitness is likely to occur if you undertake regular sporting activities.

        True   False   [1]

Total Marks _____ / 14

Energy Use, Diet, Nutrition and Hydration

1 (Circle) the correct answers.

a) Carbohydrates provide a quick supply of energy.

               True   False   [1]

b) Carbohydrates should make up approximately 60% of a sports person's diet.

               True   False   [1]

c) Pasta, brown rice and bananas are good sources of carbohydrate.

               True   False   [1]

d) The main role of protein is to provide energy.

               True   False   [1]

e) Sprinters require protein to aid performance.

               True   False   [1]

f) Having too much water causes dehydration.

               True   False   [1]

g) Chicken, fish and red meat are all foods that are high in fibre.

               True   False   [1]

2 (Circle) the correct answer for each statement.

a) Having a diet with large quantities of saturated fats can cause dangerous illnesses.

               True   False   [1]

b) It is important and beneficial to health to have a diet with some saturated fats.

               True   False   [1]

c) An athlete needs 55% of their diet to be made up of fats.

               True   False   [1]

3 Match each factor that affects optimum weight with the correct description. One has been done for you.

Sex	Big, well-toned muscles can weigh a lot without the person being overweight.
Height	An individual's weight can vary; some people are more naturally heavily built as they have heavier bones – it does not automatically mean that they are overweight.
Bone structure	Men usually have a greater optimum weight than women of the same height.
Muscle girth	Usually, the taller you are, the more you should weigh.

[3]

4 Participants in various sports tend to have different optimum weights.

Label the pictures using the following terms: endomorph, mesomorph, ectomorph.

SOMATOTYPES

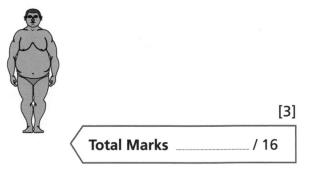

[3]

Total Marks _____ / 16

Classification of Skills

1 Continua can be used to classify skills. Circle the correct responses below.

a) A penalty kick in football.

Open skill   Closed skill   [1]

b) A gymnast completing a somersault.

Simple skill   Complex skill   [1]

c) A swimmer using front crawl.

Low organisation   High organisation   [1]

2) Match each practice method with the correct description. One has been done for you.

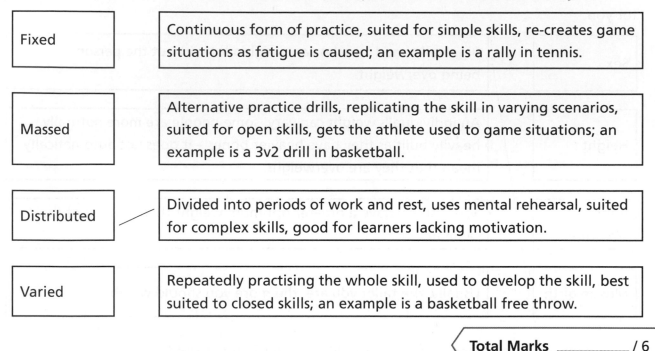

Fixed	Continuous form of practice, suited for simple skills, re-creates game situations as fatigue is caused; an example is a rally in tennis.
Massed	Alternative practice drills, replicating the skill in varying scenarios, suited for open skills, gets the athlete used to game situations; an example is a 3v2 drill in basketball.
Distributed	Divided into periods of work and rest, uses mental rehearsal, suited for complex skills, good for learners lacking motivation.
Varied	Repeatedly practising the whole skill, used to develop the skill, best suited to closed skills; an example is a basketball free throw.

[3]

Total Marks _____ / 6

Goal Setting, SMART Targets and Information Processing

1) Identify three reasons why athletes set SMART targets.

_____

_____

_____ [3]

2) Fill in the gaps.

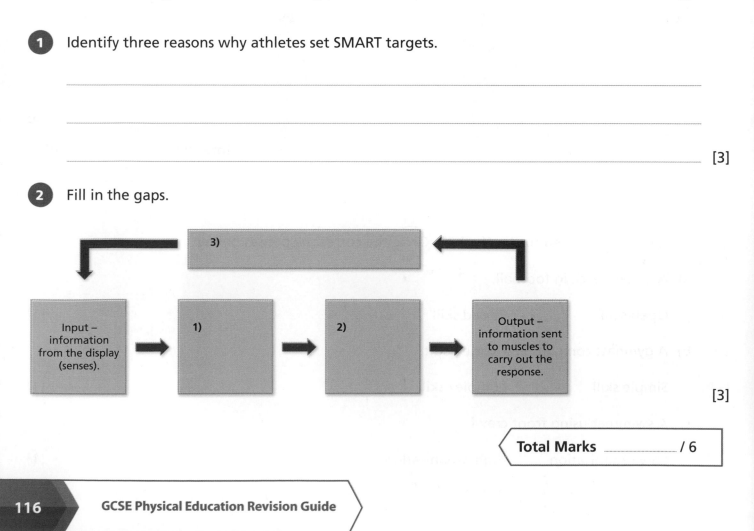

[3]

Total Marks _____ / 6

Guidance and Feedback on Performance

1 Identify two advantages of using visual guidance when coaching.

_____

_____

_____

_____ [2]

2 Identify two disadvantages of manual guidance when coaching.

_____

_____

_____

_____ [2]

Total Marks _____ / 4

Mental Preparation, Arousal and Personality

1 Explain why mental rehearsal is used as part of the warm-up.

_____

_____ [1]

2 Identify three characteristics of an extrovert.

_____

_____

_____ [3]

Total Marks _____ / 4

Review Questions

Engagement Patterns of Different Social Groups in Physical Activity and Sport

1 Explain how rates of participation in sport are affected for different social groups.

Gender:

_____

_____

_____

_____

_____ [3]

Age:

_____

_____

_____

_____ [3]

Socio-economic group:

_____

_____

_____

_____ [3]

Ethnicity:

_____

_____

_____

_____

_____

_____ [3]

Disability:

_____

_____

_____

_____

_____

_____ [3]

Total Marks _____ / 15

Commercialisation of Physical Activity and Sport

1 Explain the advantages and disadvantages of the commercialisation of a sport for the sponsor.

Advantages:

_____

_____

_____

_____ **[2]**

Disadvantages:

_____

_____

_____

_____ **[2]**

2 Explain the advantages and disadvantages of media involvement for a sport.

Advantages:

_____

_____

_____

_____ **[2]**

Disadvantages:

_____

_____

_____

_____ **[2]**

Total Marks _____ / 8

Ethical and Socio-cultural Issues in Physical Activity and Sport

1 Complete the sentences by using the missing words.

Sportsmanship	Gamesmanship	Deviance

_____ is playing within the rules, laws and regulations of the sport but pushing them to their maximum boundaries. [1]

_____ is the deliberate breaking of rules, laws or regulations of a sport. [1]

_____ is playing honestly, respecting team mates, opponents, spectators and sporting officials. [1]

2 Identify the reasons for deviance in elite sport.

_____

_____

_____ [3]

3 Identify the consequences of deviance in elite sport.

_____

_____

_____ [3]

> Total Marks _____ / 9

Contemporary Sport

Ava, 15, has been asked to do a presentation as part of her GCSE Physical Education Course on hooliganism in sport.

1 Identify the one statement that is **not** a reason for hooliganism in sport. Tick (✓) one answer. [1]

a) Pressure by sponsors ☐

b) Gang culture ☐

c) Frustration due to results ☐

d) Hype by the media ☐

2 Identify the one statement that is **not** a strategy to combat hooliganism in sport.
Tick (✓) one answer. [1]

a) All-seater stadia ☐

b) Segregation of fans ☐

c) Alcohol restrictions ☐

d) Increased funding due to selling of television rights ☐

3 Explain three ways in which television has negatively impacted sport.

_____

_____

_____

_____

_____

_____

_____ [3]

> **Total Marks** _____ / 5

Use of Data

1 What is primary research?

_____

_____ [1]

2 What is secondary research?

_____

_____ [1]

> **Total Marks** _____ / 2

Mixed Exam-Style Questions

1 Rory is following a six-week training programme to improve his fitness for football. The table below shows his fitness test results, which were collected during his six-week training programme.

Weeks	1	2	3	4	5	6
Grip strength	48 kg	50 kg	52 kg	55 kg	57 kg	61 kg
Sit and reach	10 cm	8 cm	7 cm	5 cm	4 cm	3 cm
Harvard step test	46 bpm	49 bpm	51 bpm	53 bpm	54 bpm	58 bpm

Analyse the data in the table to determine the trends for each fitness test.

_____

_____

_____

_____

_____

_____

_____ [3]

2 Rory wants to increase his fitness for football. His teacher suggests attending a spinning class.

State two advantages of using a spinning class to increase fitness.

_____

_____

_____

_____ [2]

3 The graph (**Figure 1**) illustrates the percentage of obese individuals in the UK and Ireland, 1995–2010.

Figure 1

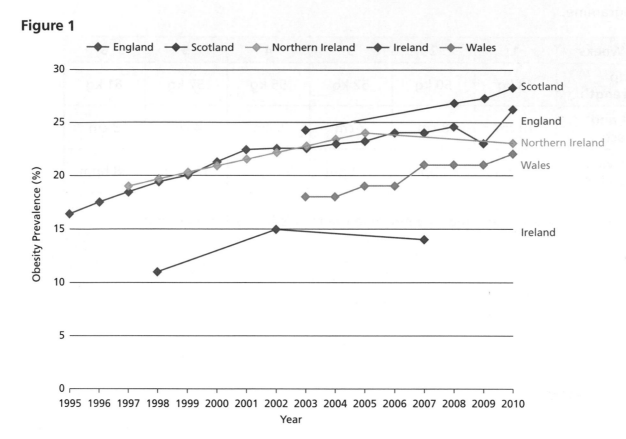

Using the graph, identify which of the following statements best describes obesity trends in the UK and Ireland. Tick (✓) one answer.

a) Obesity rates have risen.   ( )

b) Obesity rates have declined.   ( )

c) Obesity rates have stayed the same.   ( )

d) There is no clear pattern.   ( )   [1]

4 **Figure 2** shows a gymnast balancing on her tiptoes.

Figure 2

The gymnast is using a second class lever system. The toes are acting as the fulcrum at one end of the lever. The load is in the middle of the lever. Effort is at the opposite end of the lever to the fulcrum. The movement up on to the toes is the opposite to the load.

Analyse the role of the second class lever system in affecting the gymnast's performance.

_____

_____

_____

_____

_____ **[3]**

5 Choosing not to take part in physical activity is a lifestyle choice.

Explain how inactivity can impact negatively on health and well-being.

_____

_____

_____

_____

_____ **[3]**

6 Explain why the heart rate increases when a performer takes part in physical activity.

_____

_____

_____

_____

_____ **[3]**

7   Evaluate the extent to which the redistribution of blood flow is necessary during a football match.

_____

_____

_____

_____

_____

_____

_____

_____

_____

_____

_____

_____

_____

_____

_____

_____

_____

_____ [9]

8

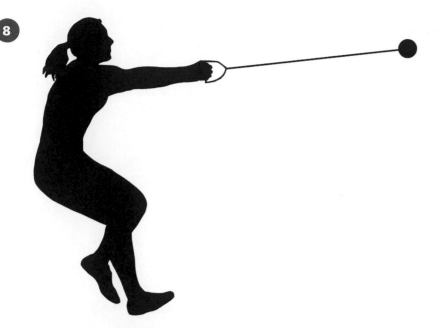

Analyse, using one example, how one of the ball and socket joints in the body allows the hammer thrower to complete the rotation.

_____

_____

_____

_____

_____

_____

_____

_____ [3]

9 Explain one role of the arteries, one role of the veins and one role of the capillaries.

_____

_____

_____

_____

_____

_____ [3]

10 Define health, fitness and exercise.

_____

_____

_____

_____

_____

_____

_____ [3]

 11 Explain the purpose of a warm-up.

_____

_____

_____

_____

_____

_____ [3]

12 Explain the phases of a warm-up.

_____

_____

_____

_____

_____

_____

_____

_____ [4]

13 Explain the role and importance of two macronutrients.

_____

_____

_____

_____

_____

_____

_____

_____ [4]

14 Explain the role and importance of two micronutrients.

_____

_____

_____

_____

_____

_____

_____ [4]

15 Evaluate whether a competitive marathon runner should use a combination of continuous training and weight training to improve their performance.

_____

_____

_____

_____

_____

_____

_____

_____

_____

_____

_____

_____

_____

_____

_____

_____

_____

_____

_____

_____

_____ [9]

16 Henry is a 15-year-old member of the school rugby team. He has just taken the Cooper 12-minute run test.

Ratings for the Cooper 12-minute run test

Age	Excellent	Above Average	Average	Below Average	Poor
Males 15–16	>2800 m	2500–2800 m	2300–2499 m	2200–2299 m	<2200 m

Which one of the following is the correct rating for Henry, given his score of 2809 m in the Cooper 12-minute run test? Tick (✓) one answer.

a) Excellent ( )

b) Above average ( )

c) Average ( )

d) Poor ( ) [1]

17 Which of the following best describes a first class lever system? Tick (✓) one answer.

a) The load and the fulcrum are at the same position on the lever. ( )

b) The load is in the middle. ( )

c) The fulcrum is in the middle of the lever. ( )

d) The load is at the right-hand end of the lever. ( ) [1]

18 Which of the following best describes sportsmanship? Tick (✓) one answer.

a) Qualities of trying to win at all costs. ( )

b) Bending the rules/laws of a sport without actually breaking them. ( )

c) Behaviour that goes against the moral values or laws of the sport. ( )

d) Qualities of fairness, following the rules, being gracious in defeat or victory. ( ) [1]

19 Explain two types of guidance a coach might use to optimise performance.

_____

_____

_____

_____

_____

_____

_____

_____

_____   [4]

20 Analyse two advantages and two disadvantages of the commercialisation of sport.

_____

_____

_____

_____

_____

_____

_____

_____

_____

_____   [4]

21 Daisy is a 16-year-old GCSE PE student. She has just taken the sit and reach test.

Ratings for the sit and reach test

	Very Poor	Poor	Fair	Average	Good	Excellent	Superior
Female	−15 cm +	−14 to 8 cm	−7 to 0 cm	1 to 10 cm	11 to 20 cm	21 to 30 cm	30 cm +

Which one of the following is the correct rating for Daisy, given her score of 9 cm in the sit and reach test? Tick (✓) one answer.

a) Excellent   ( )

b) Above average   ( )

c) Average   ( )

d) Poor   ( )   [1]

Answers

Page 5 Quick Test
1. Protection; muscle attachment; movement; produces platelets; produces white and red blood cells; storage of minerals.
2. Fixed; slightly moveable; freely moveable.
3. Long; short; flat; irregular.

Page 7 Quick Test
1. Pivot; hinge; ball and socket; condyloid.
2. Decreasing the angle at a joint.
3. Moving away from the midline of the body.

Page 9 Quick Test
1. Ligaments attach bone to bone.
2. Tendons attach muscle to bone.
3. Agonist – muscles contract; antagonist – muscles relax.
4. Type I; type IIa; type IIx.

Page 11 Quick Test
1. Arteries have thick walls and high pressure, which carries blood away from the heart. Capillaries are the small vessels that connect arteries to veins. Water, oxygen, carbon dioxide and other nutrients are exchanged in the capillaries. Veins have thin walls and low pressure and carry blood to the heart. Veins also have valves to prevent the back-flow of blood.
2. Decrease.
3. Plasma carries blood cells and platelets around the body. Red blood cells have a specific role, which is to transport oxygen around the body to the organs and muscles. Disease and infection are protected by white blood cells.

Page 13 Quick Test
1. Vital capacity is the maximum amount of air that can be breathed in or out.
2. Tidal volume is the amount of air that enters the lungs during normal breathing when at rest.
3. Aerobic respiration: (with oxygen), used in low intensity aerobic exercise, for example running a marathon. Anaerobic: (without oxygen) used in high intensity exercise, for example 100-metre running race.

Page 15 Quick Test
1. Aerobic respiration is with oxygen; anaerobic respiration is without oxygen.
2. Aerobic activity.
3. Carbohydrates fuel aerobic and anaerobic activity.

Page 17 Quick Test
1. They accumulate lactic acid, feel pain and tire quickly.
2. True.

3. Muscular system: muscles get larger; increase in strength; are able to apply more force. Respiratory system: vital capacity increases; muscles in the chest increase in strength; aerobic endurance improves. Cardio-vascular system: hypertrophy of the heart occurs – it becomes stronger and increases in size; stroke volume increases; resting heart rate decreases.

Pages 18–19 The Structure and Functions of the Musculo-skeletal System
1. a) [1]
2. c) [1]
3. d) [1]
4. Possible responses: Protects vital organs [1]; Attachment for muscle [1]; Joints for movement [1]; Produces platelets [1]; Red and white blood cell production [1]; Storage of calcium and phosphorus [1]. **(1 mark for each point made, up to a maximum of 3 marks.)**
5. Possible responses: Long bones – are longer than they are wide/have a soft centre surrounded by a hard outer casing/are used as levers to enable the body to move, examples include the ulna and tibia, the long leg bones that are used in cycling, running and swimming [1]; Short bones – are approximately as long as they are wide/have large quantities of bone marrow to make blood vessels/weight bearing, examples include the carpals and tarsals in the wrists and feet [1]; Flat bones – are flat and particularly strong/have muscles attached that provide protection, examples include the scapula (shoulder) and the cranium (skull) [1]; Irregular bones – all remaining bones are classed as irregular bones/they are often unusual in appearance/uses include both protection and muscle attachment, examples include the bones that make up the vertebral column (spine) and mandible (jaw) [1]. **(1 mark for each classification made, up to a maximum of 2 marks.)**

Pages 20–21 The Structure and Functions of the Cardio-respiratory System
1. a) [1]
2. d) [1]
3. Possible responses: Alveoli are tiny air sacs that have a large surface area [1]; Gas exchange occurs among the air sacs and their surrounding vessels [1]; Blood receives oxygen that is diffused into it [1]; Haemoglobin is contained in the red blood cells, which joins oxygen to produce ox-haemoglobin [1]; Red blood cells deliver the oxygen to muscles [1]; Carbon dioxide is removed [1]. **(1 mark for each point made, up to a maximum of 3 marks.)**

4. a) [1]
5. pulmonary artery [1]; pulmonary artery [1]; oxygen [1].
6. The number of times the heart beats in one minute. [1]
7. c) [1]

Page 22 Anaerobic and Aerobic Exercise
1. Possible responses: Muscles increase in size [1]; Muscles increase in strength [1]; Increased lactic acid tolerance [1].
2. Possible responses: Respiratory muscles increase in strength [1]; Chest cavity increases in size [1]; Vital capacity increases [1]; Increased oxygen delivery [1]; Cardio-vascular endurance improves [1]. **(1 mark for each point made, up to a maximum of 3 marks.)**
3. Possible responses: Increase in size and strength of the heart [1]; Increase in stroke volume [1]; Increase in cardiac output [1]; Resting heart rate is reduced [1]; Reduction in blood pressure [1]. **(1 mark for each point made, up to a maximum of 3 marks.)**

Page 23 The Short- and Long-term Effects of Exercise
1. True. [1]
2. Heart rate: increases, as more oxygen is needed at the muscles [1].
   Blood pressure: increases to move more blood where it is required [1].
   Stroke volume: increases to allow more blood to be pumped around the body [1].
   Cardiac output: increases to allow more blood to be pumped around the body [1].
3. d) [1]

Page 25 Quick Test
1. The fulcrum is the point of movement or pivot, generally at the centre of a joint.
2. The load is the body's weight or an external object.
3. Effort is muscular force to move the load.
4. First class lever: the fulcrum is between the effort and the load. Both effort and load move in the same direction. The pivot lies between the effort and load. An example is the place where your skull (pivot) meets the top of your spine.
   Second class lever: the fulcrum is at one end of the lever. The load is in the middle of the lever and the effort is at the opposite end of the lever to the fulcrum. The direction of effort is opposite the load; an example of this is stepping up onto your toes – the fulcrum is at the toes.
   Third class lever: the fulcrum and load are at different ends of the lever (the same as a second class lever). The effort

is off-centre on the lever, near the fulcrum. An example would be the bicep muscles, which pull the forearm towards the upper arm.

Page 27 Quick Test
1. Sagittal; frontal; transverse.
2. Frontal; sagittal; vertical.
3. Frontal axis and transverse plane.

Page 29 Quick Test
1. Fitness is the ability to meet the demands of the environment. Health is the state of physical, mental and social well-being, and includes the absence of injury and illness.
2. Exercise is a form of physical activity. Performance is how well a task is completed.
3. Cardio-vascular fitness (aerobic endurance); strength; muscular endurance; flexibility; body composition.
4. Agility; balance; coordination; power; reaction time; speed.

Page 31 Quick Test
1. Cardio-vascular fitness (aerobic endurance).
2. Cardio-vascular fitness (aerobic endurance).
3. Strength.

Page 33 Quick Test
1. Power.
2. Flexibility.
3. Speed.

Page 35 Quick Test
1. 220 – age = MHR.
2. 60–80%.
3. 80–90%.

Page 37 Quick Test
1. Strength and cardio-vascular endurance.
2. Impact on the joints.
3. 20.

Page 39 Quick Test
1. Able to train for longer and more intensely, fitness levels are improved, motor development in skills is improved, recovery is quicker, sleep better, resting heart rate is lower, blood pressure is lower, and body fat is reduced.
2. Improved bone density, improved strength of ligaments and tendons, increase in muscle hypertrophy.
3. Decrease in resting heart rate, improvements in stroke volume, increase in capilliarisation, and increase in cardiac output.

Page 41 Quick Test
1. Pre-Activity Readiness Questionnaire.
2. By using the principles of training, which can be used to prevent injury; by following the sport's rules and regulations; by using appropriate

protective clothing and equipment; by checking equipment and facilities before use.
3. Any five from: anabolic steroids; beta blockers; diuretics; narcotic analgesics; Erythropoietin (EPO); growth hormones; stimulants; blood doping.

Page 43 Quick Test
1. To prevent injury to muscles; improve the elasticity of ligaments and tendons; to increase range of movement, increase temperature and increase blood flow.
2. To remove lactic acid; to prevent DOMS; to reduce the chance of fainting or dizziness; to maintain and develop flexibility; to reduce muscle temperature; to allow heart to return to its resting rate.
3. Pulse raiser; dynamic stretching; practice activities; mental preparation.

Page 45 Quick Test
1. Quantitative research is formal and objective; it is a methodical process. Numerical data is used to obtain information, it is then analysed and differences identified.
2. Qualitative research is subjective and uses words rather than data. It looks at individual personal views and attempts to explain why, rather than what or how many.
3. According to the data Iris can be classed as excellent and has excellent cardio-vascular endurance. Edith's cardio-vascular endurance results are not as high and her fitness can be classified as above average. Finally, David's cardio-vascular endurance needs improvement as he is classed as being poor.

Pages 46–55 Practice Questions

Page 46 Lever Systems
1. c) [1]
2. c) [1]
3. Possible responses: Slow-acting movement [1]; Limited flexibility [1]

Pages 47–48 Planes and Axes of Movement
1. c) [1]
2. Possible responses: Ball and socket joints at the hip allow rotation at the hip [1]; This allows an increased range of movement [1]; Generates more power to complete the movement [1]; The ball and socket joint at the shoulder gives a complete range of movement, which means the arm can move from extension to flexion/can get the required sideways movement of the arm [1]. (1 mark for one example, 1 mark for how a ball and socket joint allows the athlete to complete the move, 1 mark for appropriate expansion of explanation, up to a total of 3 marks.)

Page 49 The Relationship between Health and Fitness
1. Fitness: the ability to meet the demands of the environment [1]; Health: the state of complete emotional, physical and social well-being, and not merely the absence of disease and infirmity [1]; Exercise: any form of physical activity done to maintain or improve health and/or fitness; it is not competitive sport [1]. (1 mark for each correct definition, 3 marks in total.)
2. Possible responses: Cardio-vascular fitness (aerobic endurance) [1]; Strength [1]; Muscular endurance [1]; Flexibility [1]; Body composition [1].

Page 50 Components of Fitness Data Interpretation
1. a) [1]
2. d) [1]
3. c) [1]

Page 51 The Principles of Training
1. Training must be raised to a higher level to create extra demands, to which the body will adapt [1]; Increase the frequency of training [1]; Increase the intensity of training [1]; Increase the amount of time you train for [1].
2. Training effects are reversible if training is not challenging or does not occur [1]; Training losses occur quicker than gains [1].
3. Possible responses: training needs to be specific to the activity/sport [1]; training needs to be the same type of fitness component [1]; training needs to take into consideration physiological and psychological make-up [1].

Pages 52–53 The Long-term Effects of Exercise
1. Possible responses: Increased bone density/stronger bones [1]; Increased strength of ligaments and tendons/better stability/thicker cartilage [1]; Muscle hypertrophy/muscles become bigger in size/fibres get thicker/stronger fibres [1]; Rest is required for adaptations [1]. (1 mark for each point, up to a maximum of 3 marks.)
2. Possible responses: Decreased resting heart rate/bradycardia [1]; Quicker recovery [1]; Increased resting stroke volume/more blood is pumped per heart beat [1]; Increased maximum cardiac output/more blood is pumped per minute [1]; Increased size/strength of heart/the heart becomes bigger and stronger [1]; Increased capillarisation/greater network of capillaries is created to assist respiration [1]; Increase in number of red blood cells/increased oxygen transfer [1]; Reduced blood pressure [1]; Increased lung

capacity/volume and vital capacity [1]; Increased alveoli/more efficient gaseous exchange [1]; Increased strength of diaphragm/increased strength of external intercostal muscles [1]. **(1 mark for each point identified, up to a maximum of 3 marks.)**
3. c) [1]
4. Possible responses: Respiratory muscles increase in strength [1]; Chest cavity increases in size [1]; Vital capacity increases [1]; Increased oxygen delivery [1]; Cardio-vascular endurance improves [1]. **(1 mark for each point identified, up to a maximum of 3 marks.)**
5. True [1]
6. False [1]
7. True [1]
8. False [1]

Page 54 How to Optimise Training and Prevent Injury
1. Play within the rules [1]; Wear the correct protective clothing [1]; Undertake safety checks before starting [1].
2. Ligaments have become stretched at a joint [1].

Page 54 Effective Use of Warm-up and Cool Down
1. Possible responses: To increase pulse [1]; To prepare muscles for dynamic activity [1]; To practise activities [1]; For mental preparation [1]. **(1 mark for each point identified, up to a maximum of 3 marks.)**

Page 55 Use of Data
1. Thomas's cardio-vascular fitness level is below average [1].
Possible responses: Methods that could be used to develop Thomas's fitness – Body pump – focuses on different muscle groups/combines weight training and aerobics/aerobic exercise [1]; Aerobics – exercising to music in a group fitness class/working aerobically [1]; Spinning – group high-intensity exercise class using bikes/aerobic exercise [1]; Continuous training – sustained aerobic exercise/minimum of 20 minutes improves cardio-vascular fitness [1]; Fartlek/speed play – incorporates changing your speed, terrain or intensity; it improves aerobic and anaerobic fitness [1]; Interval training – periods of work and relief with varying levels of intensity; it can be used to develop and improve endurance [1]. **(1 mark for identification of fitness level, 1 mark for each point made, up to a maximum of 3 marks, 4 marks available in total.)**
2. False [1]

Page 56 The Structure and Functions of the Musculo-skeletal System
1.

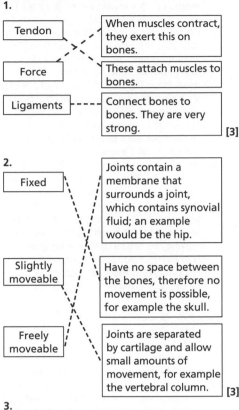

	Tendon	When muscles contract, they exert this on bones.
	Force	These attach muscles to bones.
	Ligaments	Connect bones to bones. They are very strong.

[3]

2.

	Fixed	Joints contain a membrane that surrounds a joint, which contains synovial fluid; an example would be the hip.
	Slightly moveable	Have no space between the bones, therefore no movement is possible, for example the skull.
	Freely moveable	Joints are separated by cartilage and allow small amounts of movement, for example the vertebral column.

[3]

3.

	Type I	Type IIa	Type IIx
Presence of oxygen	Oxygen present	Oxygen present	No oxygen
Colour	Red	Mainly red	White
Speed of contraction	Slow	Fast	Fastest
Resistance to fatigue: high/medium/low	Low	Medium	High
Give a sporting example	Marathon	800 metres in athletics	100-metre sprint

[5]

Pages 57–58 The Structure and Functions of the Cardio-respiratory System
1. Extension ☑; Abduction ☑; Rotation ☑; Plantar-flexion ☑. [4]
2. Stage 1: Oxygen you breathe in passes through your mouth and nose.
Stage 2: It then passes through the trachea.
Stage 3: Oxygen then enters into the bronchi and then on to the bronchioles and gases are exchanged at the alveoli.
Stage 4: Carbon dioxide exits the bronchioles and bronchi.

Stage 5: Carbon dioxide then exits the trachea.
Stage 6: Carbon dioxide then exits the mouth and nose. [6]

Page 59 Anaerobic and Aerobic Exercise
1. False [1]
2. True [1]
3. True [1]
4. False [1]

Page 59 The Short- and Long-term Effects of Exercise
1. Carbohydrates [1]; Protein [1]; Fat [1].

Page 61 Quick Test
1. Health is a state of whole physical, mental and social well-being, with the absence of disease, illness or injury.
2. Moderation; reversibility; specificity; overload; recovery; progression; tedium.
3. Frequency – how often training is undertaken; intensity – the level of training exertion; time – duration of training; type – deciding which type of training to use.

Page 63 Quick Test
1. Possible responses: Optimal sport performance; Maintain body weight; Improved health; Any other appropriate response.
2. Possible responses: Activity level; Work/rest/sleep balance; Recreational drugs; Alcohol; Nicotine.
3. True.

Page 65 Quick Test
1. 18.5–24.9.
2. Obese.
3. Increased.

Page 67 Quick Test
1. Height, bone structure and muscle girth.
2. The correct energy balance to maintain a healthy weight.

Page 69 Quick Test
1. Fixed; massed; varied; distributed.
2.

Open skills	←→	Closed skills
Simple skills	←→	Complex skills
Low organisation	←→	High organisation

3. Motor skills are related to muscle action.
4. Fine motor skills use intricate movements.
5. Gross motor skills use large muscle groups.

Answers

Page 71 Quick Test

1. To challenge, to motivate and to measure progress.
2. To increase motivation, self esteem, to reinforce the goal and to provide feedback so that new information can be used to set new goals.
3. Specific, measurable, achievable, realistic and time-based. Accept any suitable example for each stage.

Page 73 Quick Test

1. Mechanical; manual; visual; verbal.
2. Intrinsic; extrinsic; concurrent; terminal.
3. Mechanical – advantages: supports learners for dangerous skills and helps the learner understand the feel of the skill; disadvantages: learner can become reliant on the mechanical aid. Manual – advantages: good for difficult skills and improves the feel of the skill; disadvantages: learner could be uncomfortable with contact and the learner might become over-reliant on the guidance.
Visual – advantages: creates a visual image and shows the participant what the skill looks like; disadvantage: some performers might not be able to copy. Verbal – advantage: good for giving technical details; disadvantage: can be over-complicated.

Page 75 Quick Test

1. Mental preparation helps an athlete to get into a positive mindset, to focus, relax and visualise a performance going well.
2. The use of imagery to imagine a perfect performance and to help control stress.
3. True.

Pages 76–81 Practice Questions

Page 76 Physical, Emotional and Social Health, Fitness and Well-being

1. a) [1]
2. b) [1]

Page 76 The Consequences of a Sedentary Lifestyle

1. Possible responses: Depression [1]; Coronary heart disease [1]; High blood pressure [1]; Diabetes [1]; Increased risk of osteoporosis [1]; Loss of muscle tone [1]; Poor posture [1]; Poor physical fitness [1]. **(1 mark for each point, up to a maximum of 3 marks.)**

Page 77 Energy Use, Diet, Nutrition and Hydration

1. Possible responses: Break down to glucose to provide fast-release energy [1]; Carbohydrates provide energy for endurance activities/(carb load) carbohydrates in preparation for an event [1]; Build and repair muscle [1]; Power athletes such as sprinters require protein [1]; Help maintain levels of

hydration/prevent dehydration [1]; Help to avoid constipation [1]; Aid healthy digestion [1]; Help to maintain body weight [1]. **(1 mark for each point made, up to a maximum of 3 marks.)**
2. Possible responses: Help break down energy from food [1]; Required to help intensive training and competition [1]; Calcium helps strengthen bones [1]; Iodine can be used for energy production [1]; Iron prevents fatigue [1]; Vitamins are required to help the body function and aid concentration [1]; Source of slow-release energy [1]. **(1 mark for each point made, up to a maximum of 3 marks.)**
3. Performance will be reduced [1]; Can lead to death [1]; Thickness of blood increases/ viscosity increases [1]; Increase in pulse [1]; Increases pressure on heart [1]; Increase in temperature [1]; Leads to overheating [1]; Reactions are inhibited [1]; Poor decision making can occur [1]; Muscle fatigue/ cramps [1]; or any other appropriate response [1]. **(1 mark for each point made, up to a maximum of 3 marks.)**

Pages 78–79 Classification of Skills

1. a) Possible responses, open skill: The environment is constantly changing [1]; Skills are usually externally paced [1]; Open skill example: a rugby pass [1].Possible responses, closed skill: These skills take place in a stable environment [1]; Performer knows exactly what to do and when [1]; Not affected by the environment [1]; Clear beginning and end [1]; Tends to be self-paced [1]; Closed skill example: a tennis serve [1]. **(1 mark for an open skill correctly explained, 1 mark for a closed skill correctly explained, 1 mark for one example of each type of skill, 4 marks available in total.)**
   b) Possible responses, basic skill: Straightforward [1]; Requires little concentration [1]; Limited thinking required [1]; Few sub-routines [1]; Limited decision-making. Basic skill example: a chest pass in netball [1]. Possible responses, complex skill: Involves a long attention span [1]; Complicated [1]; Practised [1]; Many sub-routines [1]; Can be dangerous [1]. Complex skill example: an overhead kick in football [1]. **(1 mark for a basic skill correctly explained, 1 mark for a complex skill correctly explained, 1 mark for one example of each type of skill, 4 marks available in total.)**
   c) Possible responses, low organisation skill: Very easy [1]; Simple [1]; Sub-routines can be easily identified and isolated from the overall movement [1]; Low organisation example: front crawl in swimming [1]; Possible

responses, high organisation skill: Sub-routines are difficult to identify and isolate from the overall movement [1]; Complex [1]; Cannot be broken down into sub-routines [1]; High organisation example: golf swing [1]. **(1 mark for a low organisation skill correctly explained, 1 mark for a high organisation skill correctly explained, 1 mark for one example of each type of skill, 4 marks available in total.)**

Page 79 Goal Setting, SMART Targets and Information Processing

1. Increases motivation and resilience [1]; Reinforces goals/targets [1]; Improves confidence/self esteem [1]; Provides feedback for improvement [1]; Helps set new goals [1]; or any other suitable alternative [1] **(1 mark for each point made, up to a maximum of 2 marks.)**

Pages 80–81 Guidance and Feedback on Performance

1. a) Possible responses, visual: Definition – teacher/coach demonstrates to the learner how to do a skill/creates a visual image/uses visual aids such as video, pictures, diagrams and models [1]. Advantages: Provides mental image, shows what the skill should look like [1]; Supports verbal instruction [1]; Highlights learner error [1]. Disadvantages: Learner can lose motivation if the skill is too difficult [1]; Needs to be accurately demonstrated otherwise learning will not take place [1]; Can't copy movement [1]. **(1 mark for definition, 1 mark for a positive, 1 mark for a negative, up to a total of 3 marks.)**
   b) Possible responses, verbal: Definition – teacher/coach gives verbal instructions/often used with visual guidance/an example could be to give specific coaching points whilst giving a visual demonstration/can be used for tactics and strategies [1]. Advantages: Works well with visual guidance [1]; Good for detailed feedback for advanced performers [1]; Simple coaching points can be used for beginners [1]. Disadvantages: Amount of information needs to be limited for beginners [1]; Does not work well for complex skills [1]; Can be tedious [1]. **(1 mark for definition, 1 mark for a positive, 1 mark for a negative, up to a total of 3 marks.)**
   c) Possible responses, mechanical: Definition – teacher/coach uses equipment to aid learning, e.g. using a swimming float or a rig in trampolining. Advantages: Helps to build confidence [1]; Good for dangerous skills [1]; Breaks the skill down to make it easier to teach [1]. Disadvantages: Learner can become reliant on the aid [1];

Learner does not get a feel for the skill [1]; Can be demotivating to a learner [1]. **(1 mark for definition, 1 mark for a positive, 1 mark for a negative, up to a total of 3 marks.)**

2. Possible responses: The teacher/coach physically moves the participant's limbs or body parts [1]; Helps the learner get a feel for the skill [1]; Helps learn movement patterns [1]; For example, learning a forward roll [1]. **(1 mark for each point made, up to a maximum of 3 marks.)**

Page 81 Mental Preparation, Arousal and Personality

1. d) [1]

Pages 82–93 Review Questions

Page 82 Lever Systems

1.

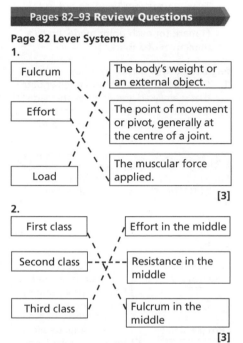

[3]

2.

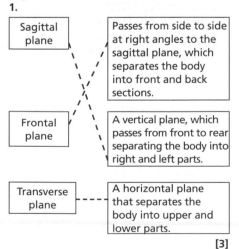

[3]

3. Advantages, any two of: Strong [1]; Stable [1]; Increasing the length of the lever will increase the mechanical advantage [1]. Disadvantages: Slow-acting movement [1]; Limited flexibility [1].

Page 83 Planes and Axes of Movement

1.

Sagittal plane	Passes from side to side at right angles to the sagittal plane, which separates the body into front and back sections.
Frontal plane	A vertical plane, which passes from front to rear separating the body into right and left parts.
Transverse plane	A horizontal plane that separates the body into upper and lower parts.

[3]

2.

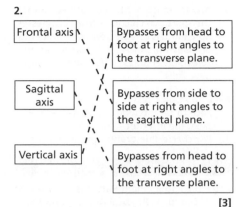

Frontal axis	Bypasses from head to foot at right angles to the transverse plane.
Sagittal axis	Bypasses from side to side at right angles to the sagittal plane.
Vertical axis	Bypasses from head to foot at right angles to the transverse plane.

[3]

Page 84 The Relationship between Health and Fitness

1. Possible responses: Reduces the chance of getting cardio-vascular disease [1]; Reduces the risk of diabetes [1]; Reduces the risk of cancer [1]; Reduces blood pressure [1]; Reduces the risk of depression [1]; Relief of stress [1]; Make friends [1]; Improved self esteem [1]. **(1 mark for each point made, up to a maximum of 5 marks.)**

2. Possible responses: Potential injury [1]; Risk of illness [1]; Loss of self esteem [1]; Bad behaviour [1]. **(1 mark for each point made, up to a maximum of 3 marks.)**

Page 85 Components of Fitness Data Interpretation

1. a) [1]
2. d) [1]
3. b) [1]

Pages 86–87 The Principles of Training

1. Training needs to be relevant to the chosen activity/sport [1]; Training needs to target same fitness component [1]; Same muscle groups need to be used [1]; Any relevant example, e.g. power training for a weightlifter [1].

2. Can lead to poor performance [1]; Could lead to the performer becoming injured [1]; Performer could become ill/unwell [1].

3. Training needs to be in the aerobic zone [1]; Heart rate needs to be 60–80% [1]; Continuous training/or steady state training should be used [1].

4. Training needs to be in the anaerobic zone [1]; Heart rate needs to be 80–90% [1]; Training needs to be performed in short, fast bursts [1]; For example, interval or fartlek training [1]; Training needs to be anaerobic where the heart cannot supply enough oxygen to the muscles [1]; If training is in the anaerobic zone, the muscles will adapt to work better without oxygen [1]. **(1 mark for each point made, up to a maximum of 3 marks.)**

Pages 87–88 The Long-term Effects of Exercise

1. Improved fitness [1]; Increased skill levels [1]; Motor development skills are improved [1]; Able to recover more quickly [1]; Improved sleep [1]; Lower resting heart rate [1]; Reduced blood pressure [1]; Low percentage of body fat [1]; Improved health [1]. **(1 mark for each point made, up to a maximum of 5 marks.)**

2. Bones become denser and stronger [1]; Ligaments become stronger [1]; Tendons become stronger [1]; Joints become more stable [1]; Articular cartilage increases in thickness [1]; Muscles become bigger in size (hypertrophy) [1]; Muscles become stronger [1]. **(1 mark for each point made, up to a maximum of 5 marks.)**

3. Possible responses: Heart rate at rest is lowered [1]; Heart becomes stronger and more efficient [1]; Recovery post-exercise is faster [1]; Resting stroke volume increases [1]; Increased maximum cardiac output [1]; The heart becomes bigger and stronger [1]; Improved network of capillaries allows improved respiration [1]; Number of red blood cells increases, which allows greater oxygen transfer [1]; Blood pressure is lower at rest [1]; Improved lung capacity/vital capacity [1]; Increased number of alveoli [1]; Stronger diaphragm and external intercostal muscles [1]. **(1 mark for each point made, up to a maximum of 6 marks.)**

Page 89 How to Optimise Training and Prevent Injury

1. Self-screening questionnaire, to be used before starting exercise [1]; Used to identify possible risk of undertaking exercise [1]; Constructed using responses to the questions [1]; Identifies a small number of individuals who need to seek further medical advice before exercising [1]; Recommendations can be made to an individual before undertaking exercise [1]. **(1 mark for identification of PARQ, 1 mark for each point made, up to 2 marks, a total of 3 marks available.)**

2. Dislocation: One of the bones at a joint is knocked out of place [1]; Sprain: Ligaments become stretched at a joint [1]; Torn cartilage: Damage to the surface area of the cartilage between bones [1].

3. Anabolic steroids [1]; Beta blockers [1]; Diuretics [1]; Narcotic analgesics [1]; Erythropoietin (EPO) [1]; Growth hormones (GH) [1]; Stimulants [1]; blood doping [1]. **(1 mark for each drug identified, up to a maximum of 5 marks.)**

Page 90 Effective Use of Warm-up and Cool Down

1. Pulse raiser [1]; Dynamic stretching [1]; Practice activities [1]; Mental preparation [1].

2. Possible responses: Remove lactic acid [1]; Prevent Delayed Onset of Muscle Soreness (DOMS) [1]; Lessen the chance of fainting [1]; Keep flexibility or improve flexibility [1]; Lower muscle

temperature **[1]**; Reduce heart rate **[1]**. **(1 mark for each point made, up to a maximum of 3 marks.)**

Pages 91–93 Use of Data

1. a) Excellent **[1]**
   b) Poor **[1]**
   c) Average **[1]**
2. a) Good **[1]**
   b) Excellent **[1]**
3. a) Poor **[1]**
   b) Below average **[1]**
4. a) 1–10% **[1]**
   b) 51–60% **[1]**
   c) 91–100% **[1]**
5. a) Above average **[1]**
   b) Excellent **[1]**
6. a) Poor **[1]**
   b) Good **[1]**
   c) Excellent **[1]**

Pages 94–103 Revise Questions

Page 95 Quick Test

1. Males
2. Young people
3. Fewer opportunities; some women fear being judged; some religious values can affect participation.

Page 97 Quick Test

1. Women and girls; the elderly; disabled people; people who are socio-economically disadvantaged; certain ethnic groups.
2. Some people are unable to afford sports equipment; some people cannot travel to a sporting venue or are unable to use sports facilities.
3. Racist behaviour can prevent individuals from taking part in sport; lack of sports classes for specific ethnic minorities; an absence of role models for some ethnic groups.

Page 99 Quick Test

1. Communication through both written and electronic forms.
2. An emphasis on making money.
3. A business-related deal.
4. No.

Page 101 Quick Test

1. Qualities of fairness, following the rules, being gracious in defeat or victory.
2. Bending the rules/laws of a sport without actually breaking them.
3. Behaviour that goes against the moral values or laws of a sport.

Page 103 Quick Test

1. Any three from: Frustration due to the result; Poor officiating; Provocation; Religion/tradition; Cheating; Importance of fixture; Late tackles in football; High tackles in rugby; Aggressive bowling in cricket; Body shots in tennis; Obstructing an opponent in basketball; High stick in hockey; or any other suitable example.
2. Any three from: To increase the chances of success; For fame; For wealth; Makes it a level playing field as many others possibly do it; or any other suitable example.

3. Any three from: Money put back into the sport, which comes from businesses; Role models can be created from being on television; Increase in participation; Television enables performers to learn new skills.

Page 105 Quick Test

1. Face to face; telephone conversations; post; the internet.
2. Bar charts; line graphs; pie charts.

Pages 106–109 Practice Questions

Page 106 Engagement Patterns of Different Social Groups in Physical Activity and Sport

1. Possible responses: Gender – fewer opportunities for women/fear of being judged/lack the confidence to take part/ some religious values do not support women taking part in sport **[1]**. Age – for young or old sport can be physically demanding/younger people don't have much time/older people often experience ill health/lack of age-specific groups/clubs can affect participation **[1]**. Socio-economic group – cannot afford equipment/ cannot afford travel to sports facilities/ cannot afford to use sports facilities **[1]**. Ethnicity – racist behaviour discourages participation/lack of sufficient specific classes/lack of role models to encourage participation **[1]**. Disability – funding can be an issue/lack of specialist coaches/ clubs/classes can affect attendance/lack of specialist facilities/lack of specialist equipment can affect attendance **[1]**. **(1 mark for each social group explained, up to a maximum of 3 marks.)**
2. a) **[1]**
3. c) **[1]**

Page 107 Commercialisation of Physical Activity and Sport

1. Possible responses: Emphasis on making money **[1]**; Can increase participation **[1]**; Increased sales/revenue **[1]**; Increased attendance **[1]**; Increased support for athletes and teams **[1]**; Events can be exaggerated by the media to help create interest and generate sales **[1]**; Dates and times of fixtures can change **[1]**; Changing of rules **[1]**; Changing of team names and stadium names **[1]**; Global interest/audience can be gained/ expanded **[1]**. **(1 mark for each point made, up to a maximum of 3 marks.)**
2. a) **[1]**
3. a) **[1]**

Page 108 Ethical and Socio-cultural Issues in Physical Activity and Sport

1. Possible responses: Sportsmanship: qualities of fairness, following the rules, being gracious in defeat or victory **[1]**. Gamesmanship: bending the rules/laws of a sport without actually breaking them **[1]**. Deviance: behaviour that goes against the moral values or laws of the sport **[1]**.

Page 109 Contemporary Sport

1. a) Possible responses: Creation of atmosphere **[1]**; Home-field advantage **[1]**; Can inspire people to take part **[1]**. **(1 mark for each point made, up to a maximum of 2 marks.)**
   b) Possible responses: Increased pressure adversely effects performer **[1]**; Potential crowd trouble **[1]**; Can affect participation by putting people off **[1]**; Safety costs/concerns **[1]**. **(1 mark for each point made, up to a maximum of 2 marks.)**
2. Possible responses: Making kick-offs earlier in the day **[1]**; All-seater stadia **[1]**; Separating fans **[1]**; Improving security **[1]**; Alcohol constraints **[1]**; Travel restrictions/banning orders **[1]**; or any other appropriate response **[1]**. **(1 mark for each point made, up to a maximum of 3 marks.)**

Page 109 Use of Data

1. Quantitative research uses number data that is analysed and findings are made **[1]**.
2. Qualitative research uses words instead of data and people's thoughts and views on a subject **[1]**.

Pages 110–121 Review Questions

Pages 110–112 Physical, Emotional and Social Health, Fitness and Well-being

1. state; physical; mental; social **[1]**
2. a) **[1]**
3. b) **[1]**
4. b) **[1]**
5.

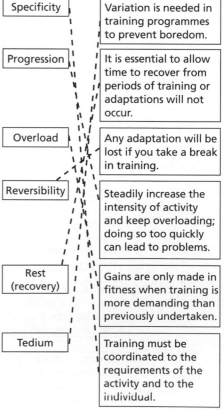

Specificity	Variation is needed in training programmes to prevent boredom.
Progression	It is essential to allow time to recover from periods of training or adaptations will not occur.
Overload	Any adaptation will be lost if you take a break in training.
Reversibility	Steadily increase the intensity of activity and keep overloading; doing so too quickly can lead to problems.
Rest (recovery)	Gains are only made in fitness when training is more demanding than previously undertaken.
Tedium	Training must be coordinated to the requirements of the activity and to the individual.

[5]

6.

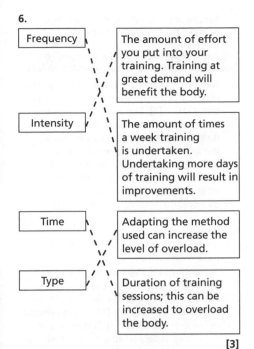

Frequency	The amount of effort you put into your training. Training at great demand will benefit the body.
Intensity	The amount of times a week training is undertaken. Undertaking more days of training will result in improvements.
Time	Adapting the method used can increase the level of overload.
Type	Duration of training sessions; this can be increased to overload the body.

[3]

7. Possible responses: Using tests and comparing data [1]; Using heart rate monitors to compare percentages of MHR [1]; Using external feedback from coaches/mentors/teachers [1]; Keeping a record/training diary and evaluating how they felt [1]; Any other suitable alternative [1]. **(1 mark for each point made, up to a maximum of 3 marks.)**

Pages 112–113 The Consequences of a Sedentary Lifestyle

1. Possible responses: Positive, any one of – aids sporting performance; helps achieve desirable body weight; health is improved [1]. Negative, any one of – increased risk of illness; increased risk of inappropriate body weight; poor physical fitness [1].
2. Positive: Can help prevent mental illness/physical illness [1]; Relief of stress [1]. Negative: Risk of injury [1]; Bad behaviour [1].
3. a) True [1]
b) False [1]
c) False [1]
d) True [1]
e) True [1]
f) True [1]
g) True [1]
h) False [1]

Pages 114–115 Energy Use, Diet, Nutrition and Hydration

1. a) True [1]
b) True [1]
c) True [1]
d) False [1]
e) True [1]
f) False [1]
g) False [1]
2. a) True [1]
b) True [1]
c) False [1]

3.

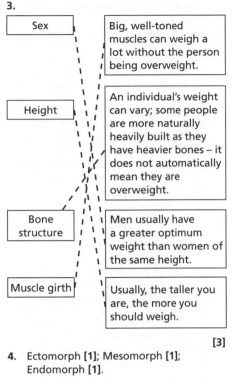

Sex	Big, well-toned muscles can weigh a lot without the person being overweight.
Height	An individual's weight can vary; some people are more naturally heavily built as they have heavier bones – it does not automatically mean they are overweight.
Bone structure	Men usually have a greater optimum weight than women of the same height.
Muscle girth	Usually, the taller you are, the more you should weigh.

[3]

4. Ectomorph [1]; Mesomorph [1]; Endomorph [1].

Pages 115–116 Classification of Skills

1. a) Closed [1]
b) Complex [1]
c) Low organisation [1]
2.

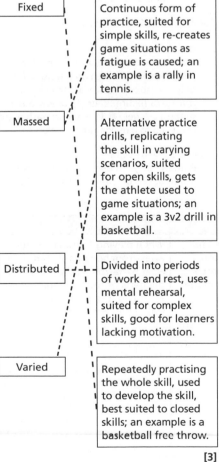

Fixed	Continuous form of practice, suited for simple skills, re-creates game situations as fatigue is caused; an example is a rally in tennis.
Massed	Alternative practice drills, replicating the skill in varying scenarios, suited for open skills, gets the athlete used to game situations; an example is a 3v2 drill in basketball.
Distributed	Divided into periods of work and rest, uses mental rehearsal, suited for complex skills, good for learners lacking motivation.
Varied	Repeatedly practising the whole skill, used to develop the skill, best suited to closed skills; an example is a basketball free throw.

[3]

Page 116 Goal Setting, SMART Targets and Information Processing

1. Improves motivation [1]; Develops confidence [1]; Provides useful feedback [1].
2.

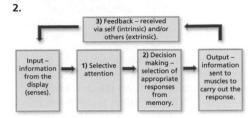

Page 117 Guidance and Feedback on Performance

1. Provides a mental image for the performer [1]; Shows the performer what the skill looks like [1].
2. Performer may become reliant on support [1]; Can prevent the learner getting a feel for the skill [1].

Page 117 Mental Preparation, Arousal and Personality

1. Helps to relax a performer/makes sure that they are sufficiently motivated [1].
2. Possible responses: Enjoy interaction with others [1]; Sociable [1]; Friendly [1]; Enthusiastic/talkative [1]; Prone to boredom when isolated/by themselves [1]; or any other appropriate response. **(1 mark for each point made, up to a maximum of 3 marks.)**

Pages 118–119 Engagement Patterns of Different Social Groups in Physical Activity and Sport

1. Gender, possible responses: Women do less sport than men [1]; There are fewer opportunities for women to do sport [1]; Some women fear being judged [1]; Some women lack the confidence to take part [1]; Opportunities for women in sport are increasing, but are still low in some areas [1]; Some religious values do not promote the participation of women in sport [1]. **(1 mark for each point made, up to a maximum of 3 marks.)**
Age, possible responses: Physically demanding sports are usually chosen by younger people, for example rugby, football and netball [1]; People that are older most often participate in sports that have less demanding strenuous impact, for example swimming and walking [1]; Younger people often cite lack of time for participation [1]; Older people often cite ill health as a reason not to participate in sport [1]; Lack of age-specific groups/clubs can affect participation [1]; In football, the introduction of veterans' walking football has helped to increase participation [1]. **(1 mark for each point made, up to a maximum of 3 marks.)**
Socio-economic group, possible responses: Some people are not able

Answers

to afford sports equipment [1]; Some people are not able to afford travel to sports locations [1]; Some people are not able to use sports facilities [1]; Some leisure providers offer a reduction in entry fees for people who are unemployed or over the age of 60 [1]. **(1 mark for each point made, up to a maximum of 3 marks.)**
Ethnicity, possible responses: Racist behaviour can prevent individuals from taking part in sport [1]; Lack of classes specifically for ethnic minorities [1]; Lack of role models [1]; Participation is increasing for ethnic minorities in sport [1]. **(1 mark for each point made, up to a maximum of 3 marks.)**
Disability, possible responses: The number of disabled people who take part in sport has risen significantly, but barriers remain [1]; Funding can be an issue [1]; Lack of specialist coaches/clubs/classes can affect attendance [1]; Lack of specialist facilities can affect attendance [1]; Lack of specialist equipment can affect attendance [1]. **(1 mark for each point made, up to a maximum of 3 marks.)**

Page 120 Commercialisation of Physical Activity and Sport

1. Advantages, possible responses: Increased publicity for the sponsor [1]; Increased sales/revenue for the sponsor [1]; Sponsor is linked to the successful team/athlete [1]; Improved image for the sponsor being associated with a successful team or individual [1]. **(1 mark for each point made, up to a maximum of 2 marks.)**
Disadvantages, possible responses: If performer/team behaves badly, the sponsor could be associated with this behaviour [1]; Performers or teams might not perform well so the sponsors do not get much recognition [1]; Performer could make negative comments on social media, which would affect the image of the sponsor [1]; Performers could change teams [1].

(1 mark for each point made, up to a maximum of 2 marks.)
2. Advantages, possible responses: Increased publicity [1]; Increased sales/revenue [1]; Increased media exposure could lead to more people participating [1]. **(1 mark for each point made, up to a maximum of 2 marks.)**
Disadvantages, possible responses: The values of the sport can be lost [1]; Events can be exaggerated to increase interest and damage reputation of the sport [1]; Media intrusion for participants [1]. **(1 mark for each point made, up to a maximum of 2 marks.)**

Page 121 Ethical and Socio-cultural Issues in Physical Activity and Sport

1. Gamesmanship [1]; Deviance [1]; Sportsmanship [1].
2. Possible responses: Focus only on winning [1]; Pressure to win [1]; Pressure from spectators [1]; Media involvement [1]; Emotional intensity of fixtures [1]; Fatigue [1]; Frustration [1]; Poor officiating [1]; Chance to win money [1]. **(1 mark for each point made, up to a maximum of 3 marks.)**
3. Possible responses: Fines [1]; Bans [1]; Negative image of participant [1]; Negative image of the sport [1]; Sponsors or commercial partners withdraw [1]; Media pressure [1]. **(1 mark for each point made, up to a maximum of 3 marks.)**

Page 121–122 Contemporary Sport

1. A
2. D
3. Attendance can be adversely affected as people chose to watch on television [1]; only mainstream sports are televised [1]; change of fixture times [1]; or any other suitable answer [1]. **(1 mark for each point made, up to a maximum of 3 marks.)**

Page 122 Use of Data

1. Primary research uses questionnaires, observations or interviews to produce data [1].

2. Secondary research uses information or data that has already been published [1].

Pages 123–132 Mixed Exam-Style Questions

1. Possible responses: The grip strength test shows an increase in strength as the score gets higher [1]; The sit and reach test is decreasing in cm, which means flexibility is declining [1]; In the Harvard step test the BPM is increasing, which suggests an increase in cardio-vascular fitness [1].
2. Performer can exercise at their own intensity level [1]; It is very good for developing aerobic endurance [1].
3. a)   [1]
4. Possible responses: Gymnasts are able to undertake small amounts of movement, which create long lever movements [1]; Fulcrum and load are at different ends of the lever [1]; However, effort is at the far end of the lever, near the fulcrum [1]; Not as effective as second class levers [1]; Gymnasts can apply a relatively small amount of effort/force from their muscles to move their relatively heavy load [1]. **(1 mark for each point made, up to a maximum of 3 marks.)**
5. Possible responses: Increased likelihood of gaining body weight [1]; Increased blood pressure [1]; Decreased bone strength [1]; Increased stress [1]; Loss of flexibility [1]; Loss of muscle tone [1]; Loss of fitness [1]; Loss of strength [1]. **(1 mark for each point made, up to a maximum of 3 marks.)**
6. Possible responses: More oxygen is needed at the muscles [1]; Stroke volume needs to increase to allow more blood to be pumped around the body [1]; Blood pressure increases as greater force from each contraction occurs [1]; Cardiac output increases to allow more blood to be pumped around the body [1]; If you cannot supply enough oxygen to your working muscles, heart rate will remain high until the oxygen debt is fully recovered [1]. **(1 mark for each point made, up to a maximum of 3 marks.)**

7.

Marks	Comments	Example of answer
3	The level of response is basic and has limited knowledge and evaluation. The response does correctly identify vasodilation, vasoconstriction and the vascular shunt mechanism. However, this knowledge is not applied to the question specifically about football and there is no conclusion.	When playing football you need to get the blood to the working muscles and away from body parts that do not require blood, for example the stomach. Your arteries narrow and this is called vasoconstriction. You also need to get blood to the parts of the body that do require blood, and this is called vasodilation. If you are doing lots of sprints when playing football, blood will need to be supplied to your leg muscles. This is called the vascular shunt mechanism.
5	Similar to the previous answer, this response appropriately identifies vasodilation, vasoconstriction and the vascular shunt mechanism. The knowledge is applied to the question about football and redistribution of blood. Also a brief conclusion is made.	When taking part in football the vascular shunt mechanism gets blood to the muscles that are working the most. Also it stops supplying as much blood to parts of the body and some organs that do not require it. Vasodilation is when your arteries expand, increasing the blood flow; the opposite of this is called vasoconstriction. When you are sprinting in football the most blood will be required at the working muscles in the legs. If you are jogging in football and the intensity is not as high, less blood will be required – and even less blood is needed if you are walking. The digestive system experiences vasoconstriction.

9	This is an excellent answer and includes all the required information, including vasodilation, vasoconstriction and the vascular shunt mechanism. The knowledge is applied to the question about football with a range of examples including walking, jogging and sprinting in relation to the redistribution of blood.	Whilst participating in a football match the pulse will increase; this is because blood moves oxygen to where it is needed the most and removes carbon dioxide where it is not needed. Breathing rate and gaseous exchange will also increase. At the working muscles where oxygen is needed arteries will vasodilate. Where oxygen is not needed, for example the stomach and digestive system, the supply will reduce. This occurs through the process of vasoconstriction. When playing football you go through periods of intense activity and periods of reduced activity. Therefore, during periods of intense activity the body will respond by increasing the blood flow around the body. When playing football and the body is in a period of reduced activity, blood flow will be significantly reduced.	
	The advantages and disadvantages of the system are highlighted. Finally, a full conclusion is made.	To conclude, when physical activity increases so does the blood flow around the body, blood will flow to where it is needed and not flow to where it is not needed. This happens through the process of vasodilation and vasoconstriction. One of the positives of this bodily system is that oxygen and nutrients will be supplied when they are needed and where they are needed. A negative of this system can be that blood pooling can occur, which might cause fainting or lactic acid accumulation. Also the system is able to match different demands when playing football, for example it will vary when walking, jogging and sprinting. However, the supply of blood to the brain will remain constant. Without redistribution of blood, players would not be able to sustain matchplay.	

8. Possible responses: Ball and socket joints at the hip allow rotation at the hip [1]; Allows a greater range of movement in the body [1]; This produces extra power to throw the hammer further [1]; The ball and socket joint at the shoulder gives a complete range of movement [1]; Therefore the athlete moves their arm from extension to flexion/can get the required sideways movement of the arm [1]; In order to throw the hammer with the correct technique/flight/follow through [1]. **(1 mark for example chosen, 1 mark for how the ball and socket joint allows the athlete to throw, 1 mark for appropriate expansion of explanation.)** Other possible responses: Hip/shoulder [1]; Specific range of movement utilised [1]; Applied to throw [1]. **(1 mark for example chosen, up to 2 marks for appropriate expansion of explanation.)**

9. Possible responses: Arteries – carry oxygenated blood away from the heart/made up of three layers with the outside being the strongest/the largest of the vessels [1]; Veins – carry deoxygenated blood/carry blood towards the heart [1]; Capillaries – are the smallest vessels/that form a network all over the body/which connects veins and arteries [1]. **(1 mark for each point made, one point should be made for each of arteries/capillaries/veins, up to a maximum of 3 marks.)**

10. Possible responses (similar will be accepted): Health – a state of complete emotional, physical and social well-being, and not merely the absence of disease and infirmity [1]; Fitness – the ability to meet the physical demands of the environment [1]; Exercise – form of physical activity done to maintain or improve health and/or fitness/it is not competitive sport [1]. **(1 mark for each point made, one point should be made for each of health/fitness/exercise, up to a maximum of 3 marks.)**

11. Possible responses: Prevent injury to muscles [1]; Improve elasticity of ligaments, tendons [1]; Increase range of movement [1]; Increase temperature of muscles [1]; Increase blood flow [1]; Prepare the body for specific exercise [1]. **(1 mark for each point made, up to a maximum of 3 marks.)**

12. Possible responses: Stage 1 – Light running/jogging/specific pulse raising for activity [1]; Increase pulse [1]; Increase blood flow [1]; Raise muscle and body temperature [1]. Stage 2 – Dynamic stretching [1]; Improve movement patterns [1]; Improved range of movement [1]. Stage 3 – Practice exercises for specific activity [1]; Warm up muscle groups relevant to activity [1]. Stage 4 – Mental preparation, visualise a good performance [1]. **(1 mark for each point made, up to a maximum of 4 marks.)**

13. Possible responses: Carbohydrates – Provide quick energy/fast-release energy [1]; should be 60% of an athlete's diet [1]; Broken down to glucose to provide fast-release energy [1]; Include foods such as cereal, bread, potatoes, rice (or any other suitable alternative) [1]; Athletes will consume (carb-load) carbohydrates in preparation for an event [1]. Protein – Builds and repairs muscle [1]; Athletes only need 15% protein in their diet [1]; Athletes will consume more protein to aid recovery/ after competition/after training [1]; Power athletes such as sprinters require protein (or any suitable alternative) [1]; Can be made up of meat, fish and pulses (or any suitable alternative) [1]. Water – helps to maintain levels of hydration [1]; Prevents dehydration [1]; It is important not to drink too much water or hypernatremia can be caused, which can be fatal as levels of salt and sodium can become dangerously low [1]. Fibre – Is indigestible and helps prevent constipation [1]; Aids healthy digestion [1]; Helps maintain body weight [1]; Source can be from whole-grain cereals, fruit and vegetables (or any suitable alternative) [1]. **(1 mark for each point made, a maximum of 2 marks given for each macronutrient, two macronutrients must be chosen.)**

14. Possible responses: Minerals – Help to break down energy from food [1]; Required to help intensive training and competition [1]; Calcium strengthens bones [1]; Iodine needed for energy production [1]; Iron prevents fatigue [1]. Vitamins – Required to help the body function [1] and aid concentration [1]; Fats – Too much saturated fat can cause heart disease [1]; Unsaturated fats are beneficial to health [1]; Are a source of slow-release energy [1]; Should be 25% of an athlete's diet [1]; Source of energy for aerobic exercise [1]; Sources include dairy, fish, nuts and oils (or any suitable alternative) [1]. **(1 mark for each point made, a maximum of 2 marks given for each micronutrient, two micronutrients must be chosen.)**

Answers

15.

Marks	Comments	Example of answer
1	The level of response is poor and has limited knowledge. The response mostly just repeats the question, which you would not get credit for.	A marathon runner should use both continuous training and weight training to build strength and aerobic endurance. This will help improve their performance as they will be stronger aerobically.
6	In comparison to the previous answer, this answer includes some detailed technical knowledge that is applied well. However the answer fails to evaluate either of the methods effectively or to make a conclusion.	An elite marathon runner needs to have an extremely well-developed aerobic threshold and anaerobic threshold. The aerobic threshold helps the athlete when working aerobically. The elite runner will want to increase their aerobic threshold because this will mean that they are able to run faster for longer. If they go above their aerobic zone of 70–80% of their maximum heart rate, they will move into their anaerobic zone. When they are above this threshold and into the anaerobic threshold activity cannot be sustained for long. Continuous training is very good for marathon training as it matches the demands of the sport and the same muscle groups are used. Elite athletes need to do more than just running for their training, they need to have strength as well to help maintain form during endurance events and to help prevent injuries. By using runner-specific strength-training workouts an athlete can improve the strength of ligaments, tendons and muscles, and this will help with enduring the impact of running. Strength training can help improve overall performance – adding heavy resistance exercises, in particular, can make you faster during the final sprint of a race.
9	This is an excellent answer that includes all the required information. It has good levels of knowledge, which are displayed throughout and applied. Evaluation of both methods of training is used and an appropriate conclusion is made.	A world-class runner needs to have an exceptionally well-established aerobic threshold and anaerobic threshold. An elite athlete needs to have an excellent aerobic threshold. Having a well-developed aerobic threshold means that an athlete can perform optimally using oxygen, meaning they are able to run quicker for longer periods of time. If an athlete goes above their 70–80% aerobic zone, he/she will move into their anaerobic zone. This can be calculated using maximum heart rate. Once in the anaerobic threshold zone the athlete cannot continue for very long. Continuous training is very good for marathon training as it matches the demands of the sport and the same muscle groups are used. Running can be tedious so it is important to introduce variety into training, which can be done through doing fartlek, interval or continuous training. The athlete can use each type of training to achieve set objectives, for example one of the advantages of continuous training is that it can be used specifically to improve aerobic and anaerobic thresholds. In addition, other advantages of this type of training are that minimal amounts of equipment are required and it can also be good for helping to achieve ideal body weight. One of the disadvantages of interval and fartlek training is that it can be very hard to maintain effort when fatigue occurs. Elite athletes need to do more than just running as their training, they need to build strength as well to help maintain form during endurance events and to help prevent injuries. By using runner-specific strength-training workouts an athlete can improve the strength of ligaments, tendons and muscles so that they can endure the impact of running. Strength training can help improve overall performance, and adding heavy resistance exercises, in particular, can make you faster during the final sprint of a race. One of the advantages of undertaking strength training is that particular muscles can be targeted and adapted to the needs of runners. Negatively, muscle soreness can occur and prevent training. Also, when an athlete builds muscle they might gain weight, which is detrimental to performance as being heavier will require more effort. There are many positives and negatives of undertaking continuous training and weight training to improve performance. However, they are both essential methods to improve results and achieve high-level performance.

16. a) [1]

17. c) [1]

18. d) [1]

19. Possible responses: Visual – Coach demonstrates to the learner how to do a skill [1]; Creates a visual image [1]; Visual aids could include videos, pictures, diagrams and models [1]. Verbal – Teacher/coach gives verbal instructions [1]; Often used with visual guidance [1]; Can be used for tactics and strategies [1]. Manual – Teacher/coach physically manipulating the learner's body [1]; Through the correct movement pattern [1]; Teacher/coach supporting a learner [1]. Mechanical – Teacher/coach uses equipment to aid learning [1]; For example using a swimming float or a rig in trampolining [1]. **(1 mark for each point made, a maximum of 2 marks given for each type of guidance, two types of guidance must be chosen.)**

20. Possible responses: Advantages – Increased awareness [1]; Increased publicity [1]; Increased sales/revenue [1]; Product linked to successful athlete/team [1]; Free clothing/equipment for team/performer [1]; Reduce financial worries for team/club/performer [1]; Professional support can be provided [1]; Merchandise available [1]. Disadvantages – If performer/team behaves badly then they can be associated with the sponsor and damage their image [1]; Dates/times of fixtures changed [1]; Teams tied to wearing specific clothing/kit [1]; Player/performer tied to wearing specific clothing/kit [1]; Commercial sponsor appearances can affect performance and training [1]; Changing of stadium and competition names [1]; Changing of team names [1]. **(1 mark for each point made, a maximum of 2 marks for two advantages and 2 marks for two disadvantages.)**

21. c) [1]

Glossary and index

Collins

GCSE Revision

Physical Education

GCSE

Workbook

Matthew Fleet

Revision Tips

Rethink Revision

Have you ever taken part in a quiz and thought *'I know this!'* but, despite frantically racking your brain, you just couldn't come up with the answer?

It's very frustrating when this happens but, in a fun situation, it doesn't really matter. However, in your GCSE exams, it will be essential that you can recall the relevant information quickly when you need to.

Most students think that revision is about making sure you **know** *stuff*. Of course, this is important, but it is also about becoming confident that you can **retain** that *stuff* over time and **recall** it quickly when needed.

Revision That Really Works

Experts have discovered that there are two techniques that help with all of these things and consistently produce better results in exams compared to other revision techniques.

Applying these techniques to your GCSE revision will ensure you get better results in your exams and will have all the relevant knowledge at your fingertips when you start studying for further qualifications, like AS and A Levels, or begin work.

It really isn't rocket science either – you simply need to:

- **test yourself** on each topic as many times as possible
- **leave a gap** between the test sessions.

Three Essential Revision Tips

1. **Use Your Time Wisely**

   - Allow yourself plenty of time.
   - Try to start revising at least six months before your exams – it's more effective and less stressful.
   - Your revision time is precious so use it wisely – using the techniques described on this page will ensure you revise effectively and efficiently and get the best results.
   - Don't waste time re-reading the same information over and over again – it's time-consuming and not effective!

2. **Make a Plan**

   - Identify all the topics you need to revise (this All-in-One Revision & Practice book will help you).
   - Plan at least five sessions for each topic.
   - One hour should be ample time to test yourself on the key ideas for a topic.
   - Spread out the practice sessions for each topic – the optimum time to leave between each session is about one month but, if this isn't possible, just make the gaps as big as realistically possible.

3. **Test Yourself**

   - Methods for testing yourself include: quizzes, practice questions, flashcards, past papers, explaining a topic to someone else, etc.
   - This All-in-One Revision & Practice book provides seven practice opportunities per topic.
   - Don't worry if you get an answer wrong – provided you check what the correct answer is, you are more likely to get the same or similar questions right in future!

Visit our website to download your free flashcards, for more information about the benefits of these techniques, and for further guidance on how to plan ahead and make them work for you.

www.collins.co.uk/collinsGCSErevision

Contents

Applied Anatomy and Physiology

Movement Analysis

Physical Training

Health, Fitness and Well-being

Sport Psychology

Socio-cultural Influences

1 Describe what a joint is.

_____

_____ [1]

2 Identify **four** functions of the skeleton.

_____

_____

_____

_____ [4]

3 Explain the structure of a long bone.

_____

_____

_____

_____

_____

_____ [3]

4 Explain the role of platelets, red blood cells and white blood cells.

_____

_____

_____

_____

_____

_____ [3]

Total Marks _____ / 11

The Structure and Functions of the Musculo-skeletal System 2

1 Describe the **three** main types of joints.

_____

_____

_____

_____

_____

_____

[3]

2 Describe the role and function of the ball and socket joint.

_____

_____

_____

_____

_____

_____

[3]

3 Explain the term flexion.

_____

_____

[1]

Total Marks _____ / 7

The Structure and Functions of the Musculo-skeletal System 3

1 Describe the characteristics of slow twitch muscle fibres (Type I).

_____

_____

_____

_____

_____

_____

_____

_____

[4]

2 Describe the characteristics of type IIx muscle fibres.

_____

_____

_____

_____

_____

_____

_____

_____

[4]

Total Marks _____ / 8

The Structure and Functions of the Cardio-respiratory System 1

1 Explain the function of capillaries and veins.

a) Capillaries: _____

_____ [1]

b) Veins: _____

_____ [1]

2 Explain the structure of the cardio-vascular system.

_____

_____

_____

_____

_____

_____

_____

_____

_____ [5]

3 Explain the function of vasodilation and vasoconstriction.

a) Vasodilation: _____

_____ [1]

b) Vasoconstriction: _____

_____ [1]

Total Marks _____ / 9

The Structure and Functions of the Cardio-respiratory System 2

1 At rest and during exercise the cardiovascular and respiratory systems work together to enable the body to function. Explain how the process works.

_____

_____

_____

_____

_____

_____

_____

_____

[4]

2 Explain how the cardio-vascular and respiratory systems change when physical activity or sport starts.

_____

_____

_____

_____

_____

[3]

3 Explain the structure of the alveoli.

_____

_____

_____

_____

_____

[3]

Total Marks _____ / 10

Anaerobic and Aerobic Exercise

1 Explain anaerobic exercise.

_____

_____

_____

_____

_____

_____

_____

_____ [3]

2 Explain aerobic respiration.

_____

_____

_____

_____

_____

_____

_____

_____ [4]

3 Identify **three** different energy sources for fuelling the body for physical activity or sport.

_____

_____

_____ [3]

Total Marks _____ / 10

The Short- and Long-term Effects of Exercise

1 Explain the short-term effects of exercising on lactic acid accumulation and muscle fatigue.

_____

_____

_____

_____

_____

_____ [3]

2 Identify the short-term effects of exercising on heart rate, stroke volume and cardiac output.

_____

_____

_____

_____

_____ [3]

3 Explain how the respiratory and cardio-vascular systems work together when exercising.

_____

_____

_____

_____

_____

_____

_____

_____ [4]

Total Marks _____ / 10

Lever Systems

1 Define the terms fulcrum, load and effort.

_____

_____

_____

_____

_____

_____ [3]

2 Which of these is an example of second class lever? Tick (✓) one answer.

a) The neck pivoting ( )

b) Lower leg on tiptoes ( )

c) The jaw opening ( )

d) The forearm flexing ( ) [1]

3 Analyse the use of third class levers in sport and physical activity.

_____

_____

_____

_____

_____

_____ [3]

Total Marks _____ / 7

Planes and Axes of Movement

1 Define the body's **three** different planes of movement.

_____

_____

_____

_____

_____

_____

[3]

2 Define the body's **three** different axes of movement.

_____

_____

_____

_____

_____

_____

[3]

3 Using an example, explain how the body's planes and axes can affect sports movement.

_____

_____

_____

_____

_____

[2]

Total Marks _____ / 8

The Relationship between Health and Fitness

1 Identify the correct definition of fitness. Tick (✓) one answer.

    a) The ability to meet the physical demands required for sport or physical activity.   ( )

    b) The ability to remain calm under pressure when required for sport or physical activity.   ( )

    c) Completing a physical task efficiently.   ( )

    d) Having good muscular endurance.   ( )   **[1]**

2 Identify the correct definition of health. Tick (✓) one answer.

    a) The ability to be highly motivated for sport and physical activity.   ( )

    b) Undertaking physical exertion to improve cardiovascular fitness.   ( )

    c) Completing a physical task efficiently.   ( )

    d) The state of physical, mental and social well-being and being free from injury and illness.   ( )   **[1]**

3 Stefanie's level of health, fitness and exercise can affect her ability to lead a healthy, active lifestyle.

Explain how Stefanie can improve her physical health.

_____

_____

_____

_____

_____

_____   **[3]**

> **Total Marks** _____ / 5

Components of Fitness Data Interpretation 1

Grip dynamometer test

This test measures strength.

Normative data, 16–19 year-olds

Gender	Excellent	Good	Average	Fair	Poor
Male	>56	51–56	45–50	39–44	<39
Female	>36	31–36	25–30	19–24	<19

Using the table above correctly identify the level of fitness for the following individuals.
Tick (✓) one answer for each question.

 1   Dennis, who is a 19-year-old male, has a score of 32.

     a) excellent   ( )

     b) good   ( )

     c) fair   ( )

     d) poor   ( )   [1]

2   Julie, who is an 18-year-old female, has a score of 42.

     a) excellent   ( )

     b) good   ( )

     c) fair   ( )

     d) poor   ( )   [1]

3   Betsy, who is a 16-year-old female, has a score of 36.

     a) excellent   ( )

     b) good   ( )

     c) fair   ( )

     d) poor   ( )   [1]

Total Marks _____ / 3

Components of Fitness Data Interpretation 2

One-minute press-up test

This test measures muscular endurance.

Normative data, 18–25 year-olds

Male 18–25	
Excellent	>56
Good	47–56
Above average	35–46
Average	19–34
Below average	11–18
Poor	4–10
Very poor	<4

Female 18–25	
Excellent	>35
Good	27–35
Above average	21–26
Average	11–20
Below average	6–10
Poor	2–5
Very poor	<2

Using the table above correctly identify the level of fitness for the following individuals.
Tick (✓) one answer for each question.

1 Brian, who is a 24-year-old male, has a score of 20.

 a) excellent ( )

 b) good ( )

 c) average ( )

 d) poor ( ) [1]

2 Gabi, who is an 18-year-old female, has a score of 36.

 a) excellent ( )

 b) good ( )

 c) average ( )

 d) poor ( ) [1]

Total Marks _____ / 2

The Principles of Training 1

1 Explain the **five** principles of training.

_____

_____

_____

_____

_____

_____

_____

_____

_____

_____

[5]

2 Shelley, who is 20, wants to improve her cardio-vascular endurance.

Explain how and why she would use the simple maximum heart rate formula.

_____

_____

_____

_____

_____

[3]

Total Marks _____ / 8

The Principles of Training 2

1 A body pump class has many advantages and disadvantages.

a) Explain **three** advantages of a body pump class.

_____

_____

_____

_____

_____

_____   [3]

b) Explain **two** disadvantages of a body pump class.

_____

_____

_____

_____   [2]

2 There are many advantages of undertaking an aerobics class.

Explain **four** advantages of an aerobics class.

_____

_____

_____

_____

_____

_____

_____

_____   [4]

Total Marks _____ / 9

The Long-term Effects of Exercise

1 There are many benefits of undertaking long-term exercise for an individual. Explain **four** long-term effects.

_____

_____

_____

_____

_____

_____

_____

_____

[4]

2 Explain how improved bone density, strength of ligaments and tendons, and muscle hypertrophy can improve performance in physical activity and sport.

a) Bone density:

_____

_____

[1]

b) Strength of ligaments and tendons:

_____

_____

[1]

c) Muscle hypertrophy:

_____

_____

[1]

Total Marks _____ / 7

How to Optimise Training and Prevent Injury

1 Explain why and how a fitness instructor would use a Pre-Activity Readiness Questionnaire (PARQ).

_____

_____

_____

_____

_____ [3]

2 Explain how the following common injuries can occur in physical activity and sport.

a) Concussion:

_____

_____ [1]

b) Dislocation:

_____

_____ [1]

c) Sprain:

_____

_____ [1]

d) Fractures:

_____

_____ [1]

e) Abrasions:

_____

_____ [1]

Total Marks _____ / 8

Effective Use of Warm-up and Cool Down

1. Before Tom competes in his 100-metre running race he undertakes an extensive warm-up so that he is physiologically prepared.

   Explain why Tom completes his warm-up.

   _____

   _____

   _____

   _____

   _____

   _____ [3]

2. Explain the reasons Tom would complete a cool down after his 100-metre race.

   _____

   _____

   _____

   _____

   _____

   _____ [3]

3. Describe what an athlete would do during each stage of a warm-up.

   a) Stage 1:

      _____ [1]

   b) Stage 2:

      _____ [1]

   c) Stage 3:

      _____ [1]

   d) Stage 4:

      _____ [1]

Total Marks _____ / 10

Use of Data

Kirsty and Dylan have undertaken a series of fitness tests as part of their GCSE Physical Education coursework. They undertook three fitness tests: the Cooper 12-minute run test, which measures aerobic endurance, the grip dynamometer test, which measures strength, and the sit and reach test, which measures flexibility.

Table 1: Cooper 12-minute run test: normative data

Age	Excellent	Above average	Average	Below average	Poor
Males 15–16	> 2800 m	2500–2800 m	2300–2499 m	2200–2299 m	< 2200 m
Females 15–16	> 2100 m	2000–2100 m	1700–1999 m	1600–1699 m	< 1600 m

1 Using the information in **Table 1**, what classification would Dylan be with a score of 2345 metres? Tick (✓) one answer.

a) Excellent ( )

b) Above average ( )

c) Average ( )

d) Poor ( ) [1]

2 Using the information in **Table 1**, what classification would Kirsty be with a score of 2555 metres? Tick (✓) one answer.

a) Excellent ( )

b) Above average ( )

c) Average ( )

d) Poor ( ) [1]

Total Marks _____ / 2

Physical, Emotional and Social Health, Fitness and Well-being

1 Define the term health.

_____

_____ [1]

2 Define the term social health.

_____

_____ [1]

3 Jordan plays football for his county team. To maximise the performance of the team, the coach develops a training programme, using the FITT principles.

For each change the coach makes below tick (✓) one answer to identify the FITT principle being used.

   a) Increasing the amount of times Jordan trains a week from 3 to 4.

      i) frequency   ( )

      ii) intensity   ( )

      iii) time   ( )

      iv) type   ( )   [1]

   b) Increasing the length of training sessions from 60 minutes to 75 minutes.

      i) frequency   ( )

      ii) intensity   ( )

      iii) time   ( )

      iv) type   ( )   [1]

   c) Increasing the levels of exertion in the training session.

      i) frequency   ( )

      ii) intensity   ( )

      iii) time   ( )

      iv) type   ( )   [1]

Total Marks _____ / 5

1 Diet and activity level can have both positive and negative impacts on health, well-being and fitness.

Explain how they can have a positive impact and a negative impact for participants.

a) Diet

Positive impact:

_____

_____

_____ [1]

Negative impact:

_____

_____

_____ [1]

b) Activity level

Positive impact:

_____

_____

_____ [1]

Negative impact:

_____

_____

_____ [1]

Total Marks _____ / 4

The Consequences of a Sedentary Lifestyle 2

1 What are the consequences of being overweight and having a sedentary lifestyle?

_____

_____

_____

_____

_____

_____

_____

_____

_____

_____

_____ [5]

2 Having a body mass index (BMI) of 40+ would classify an individual as…? Tick (✓) one answer.

a) Healthy ( )

b) Overweight ( )

c) Underweight ( )

d) Severely obese ( ) [1]

3 Having a body mass index (BMI) of 15 would classify an individual as…? Tick (✓) one answer.

a) Healthy ( )

b) Overweight ( )

c) Underweight ( )

d) Severely obese ( ) [1]

Total Marks _____ / 7

Energy Use, Diet, Nutrition and Hydration

1 Laura has started going to an aerobics class at her local leisure centre. To improve her performance, she has decided to improve her diet. Laura has identified that she needs to consume a range of macronutrients and micronutrients.

Explain why Laura needs to consume the following macronutrients:

a) Carbohydrates:

_____

_____

_____

_____ [2]

b) Protein:

_____

_____

_____

_____ [2]

2 Explain why Laura needs to consume the following micronutrients: vitamins.

_____

_____

_____

_____ [2]

3 Identify **three** factors that affect optimum body weight.

_____

_____

_____

_____ [3]

Total Marks _____ / 9

Classification of Skills

1. Various classifications can be used to categorise sports movements.

   Identify examples for the open and closed, and simple and complex continua.

   a) Open and closed continua

   Open example:

   _____ [1]

   Closed example:

   _____ [1]

   b) Simple and complex continua

   Simple example:

   _____ [1]

   Complex example:

   _____ [1]

2. Explain how fixed and massed practice can be used by a coach.

   _____

   _____

   _____

   _____

   _____

   _____

   _____

   _____ [4]

Total Marks _____ / 8

Goal Setting, SMART Targets and Information Processing

A new head coach has recently been appointed at Michael's rugby club. The new coach is keen to develop the team physiologically and psychologically to improve performance for the forthcoming season. The coach wants to get individuals to use goal setting and SMART targets.

1 Explain how SMART targets can help a performer.

_____

_____

_____

_____

_____ [3]

2 Using an example, explain how each SMART stage can be applied to improve performance.

a) Specific:

_____

_____ [1]

b) Measurable:

_____

_____ [1]

c) Achievable:

_____

_____ [1]

d) Realistic:

_____

_____ [1]

e) Time-based:

_____

_____ [1]

Total Marks _____ / 8

Guidance and Feedback on Performance

1   Various forms of guidance can be used by coaches and physical education teachers to support the learning of new sports skills.

Explain **one** advantage of each type of guidance.

   a) Visual:

   _____

   _____   [1]

   b) Verbal:

   _____

   _____   [1]

2   Explain **one** disadvantage of each type of guidance.

   a) Mechanical:

   _____

   _____   [1]

   b) Manual:

   _____

   _____   [1]

3   Identify the **four** types of feedback.

   _____

   _____

   _____

   _____   [4]

Total Marks _____ / 8

Mental Preparation, Arousal and Personality

1 Mannie competes in the long jump for his county. To help with his jumps prior to competing he uses mental preparation.

Explain why Mannie would use mental preparation before jumping as part of his warm-up.

_____

_____

_____

_____

_____

_____

_____

_____   [4]

2 Define mental rehearsal.

_____

_____

_____

_____   [1]

Total Marks _____ / 5

1 Use **Figure 1** to explain engagement patterns for females.

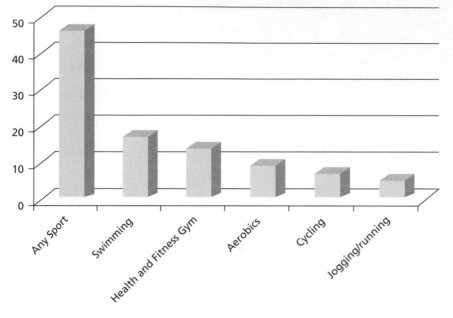

Figure 1

Female Participation in Sport

_____

_____

_____

_____

_____

[3]

2 Various different groups have low levels of participation in physical activity and sport. Explain the reasons why minority ethnic groups may have low levels of participation in sport.

_____

_____

_____

_____

_____

[3]

Total Marks _____ / 6

Engagement Patterns of Different Social Groups in Physical Activity and Sport 2

1 Explain socio-economic factors that could affect an individual's participation in sport.

_____

_____

_____

_____

_____

_____

_____

_____

_____

_____

[5]

2 Explain factors that could affect a disabled individual's participation in sport.

_____

_____

_____

_____

_____

_____

_____

_____

_____

_____

[5]

Total Marks _____ / 10

Commercialisation of Physical Activity and Sport

1 Sport and commercialism are interrelated in the twenty-first century. Explain how commercialism shapes modern sport.

_____

_____

_____

_____

_____

_____

_____

_____

[4]

2 There are both advantages and disadvantages to the commercialism of sport.

Explain **two** advantages.

_____

_____

_____

_____

[2]

3 There are both advantages and disadvantages to the media being involved in sport for the player/performer.

Explain **two** disadvantages.

_____

_____

_____

_____

[2]

Total Marks _____ / 8

Ethical and Socio-cultural Issues in Physical Activity and Sport

1 Identify **four** different examples of deviance in sport.

_____

_____

_____

_____ [4]

2 Using examples to support your work, explain the term sportsmanship.

_____

_____

_____

_____

_____

_____ [2]

3 Using an example to support your work, explain the term gamesmanship.

_____

_____

_____

_____

_____ [2]

Total Marks _____ / 8

1 Explain **three** reasons for violence in sport.

_____

_____

_____

_____

_____

_____

_____ [3]

2 Explain **three** strategies employed to combat hooliganism.

_____

_____

_____

_____

_____

_____

_____ [3]

3 Television has both a positive and a negative influence on sport.

a) Identify **two** positive influences of television on sport.

_____

_____ [2]

b) Identify **two** negative influences of television on sport.

_____

_____ [2]

Total Marks _____ / 10

Use of Data

1 Fatima and William have tested their entire school year using the multi-stage fitness test. They have recorded 180 learners' results.

Which method would be best to display the **trend** in the school year? Tick (✓) one answer.

a) Bar chart ( )

b) Pie chart ( )

c) Line graph ( )

d) Data table ( ) [1]

2 Identify **four** different ways to collect data.

_____

_____

_____

_____ [4]

3 Identify **three** different ways to present data.

_____

_____

_____ [3]

Total Marks _____ / 8

Write your name here

Surname		Other names

GCSE

Physical Education
Component 1: Fitness and Body Systems

Time: 1 hour and 45 minutes	Paper Reference
	1PE0/01

You will need a calculator.	Total Marks

Instructions

- Use **black** ink or ball-point pen.
- Answer **all** questions.
- Answer the questions in the spaces provided.

Information

- The total mark for this paper is 90.
- The marks for **each** question are shown in brackets.
  - *use this as a guide as to how much time to spend on each question.*

Advice

- Read each question carefully before you start to answer it.
- Check your answers if you have time at the end.

Answer ALL questions.

Write your answers in the spaces provided.

Some questions must be answered with a cross in a box ☒. If you change your mind about an answer, put a line through the box ☒ and then mark your new answer with a cross ☒.

1   **(a)** Which one of the following muscle fibre types is best suited for a cyclist on a 3-hour ride?

☒ **A** Type I

☒ **B** Type IIa

☒ **C** Type IIx

☒ **D** Fast   (1)

(b) What classification of bone is shown in **Figure 1**?

Figure 1

☒ **A** Long

☒ **B** Short

☒ **C** Irregular

☒ **D** Flat   (1)

(c) Which of the following tests should be used to measure flexibility?

☒ **A** Cooper run

☒ **B** Sit and reach

☒ **C** Harvard step test

☒ **D** Vertical jump test (1)

(d) Which of the following tests should be used to measure power?

☒ **A** Cooper run

☒ **B** Sit and reach

☒ **C** Harvard step test

☒ **D** Vertical jump test (1)

Alan is a 16-year-old PE student. He has just completed the sit and reach test. **Table 1** shows ratings for the sit and reach test.

	Very Poor	Poor	Fair	Average	Good	Excellent	Superior
Male	–20 cm +	–19 to –9 cm	–8 to 1 cm	0 to 5 cm	6 to 16 cm	17 to 26 cm	27 cm +

Table 1

(e) Alan scored 9 cm. Which of the following best describes his score?

☒ **A** Excellent

☒ **B** Good

☒ **C** Fair

☒ **D** Poor (1)

The Stork test is used to evaluate balance. **Table 2** shows Stork test ratings.

Rating	Score (seconds)
Excellent	> 50
Good	40–50
Average	25–39
Fair	10–24
Poor	< 10

Table 2

(f) If Callum lasts 26 seconds, what word best describes his score?

☒ **A** Excellent

☒ **B** Good

☒ **C** Average

☒ **D** Poor   (1)

(g) If Heidi lasts 76 seconds, what word best describes her score?

☒ **A** Excellent

☒ **B** Good

☒ **C** Average

☒ **D** Poor   (1)

(h) Which is the correct description for tidal volume?

☒ **A** The maximum amount of air that can be breathed in or out.

☒ **B** The amount of times the heart beats in a minute.

☒ **C** The amount of oxygen you need when exercising.

☒ **D** The amount of air which enters the lungs during normal breathing when at rest.   (1)

(i) What best describes a frontal axis?

☒ **A** Bypasses from side to side at right angles to the sagittal plane

☒ **B** Bypasses horizontally from front to rear lying at right angles to the frontal plane

☒ **C** Bypasses from head to foot at right angles to the transverse plane

☒ **D** None of the above (1)

(j) What best describes the transverse plane?

☒ **A** Vertical plane which passes from front to rear separating the body into right and left parts

☒ **B** Passes from side to side at right angles to the sagittal plane, which separates the body into a front and back section

☒ **C** Horizontal plane that separates the body into upper and lower parts

☒ **D** None of the above (1)

(Total for Question 1 = 10 marks)

2   Muscles work in pairs.

Using **one** example, explain how muscles working in pairs aid physical activity and sport.

_____

_____

_____

_____

_____

_____

(Total for Question 2 = 3 marks)

3   **Figure 2** shows an Association Footballer attempting to shoot at goal.

Figure 2

Analyse how the footballer uses both the ankle joint and hip joint to strike the football.

_____

_____

_____

_____

_____

_____

(Total for Question 3 = 3 marks)

4

Figure 3

Figure 3 shows an athlete completing a bicep curl using a dumbbell.

Identify the lever used and explain how it affects movement.

_____

_____

_____

_____

_____

_____

(Total for Question 4 = 3 marks)

5   Muscles work with the skeleton to bring about specific sporting movements.

Complete **Table 3** by:

(a) stating the function of each muscle

(b) giving an example of a specific sporting movement that uses each muscle.

Muscle	(a) Function	(b) Specific sporting movement
Deltoid	(1)	(1)
Hamstring	(1)	(1)

Table 3

(Total for Question 5 = 4 marks)

6 Complete **Table 4** by:

(a) stating the function of each muscle

(b) giving an example of a specific sporting movement that uses each muscle.

Muscle	(a) Function	(b) Specific sporting movement
Gastrocnemius	(1)	(1)
Bicep	(1)	(1)

Table 4

(Total for Question 6 = 4 marks)

7

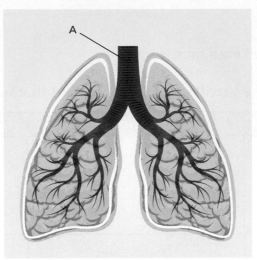

Figure 4

Complete the following statements about **Figure 4**.

The structure labelled A in **Figure 4** is the _____.

For the body to move, _____ needs to be supplied to the muscles. The lungs, blood and the _____ , work together in a continual sequence to help the flow of oxygenated and deoxygenated blood round the body.

(Total for Question 7 = 3 marks)

8 Identify the different functions of the skeleton that can be used in physical activities and sports.

_____

_____

_____

_____

_____

_____

(Total for Question 8 = 3 marks)

9 Explain **three** different classifications of bones.

_____

_____

_____

_____

_____

_____

_____

_____

(Total for Question 9 = 3 marks)

10 Identify the **three** body planes.

_____

_____

_____ (3)

(Total for Question 10 = 3 marks)

11 Identify the **three** body axes.

_____

_____

_____ (3)

(Total for Question 11 = 3 marks)

12 Explain how high altitude training can affect aerobic performance.

_____

_____

_____

_____

_____ (3)

(Total for Question 12 = 3 marks)

13 Explain how to improve aerobic threshold.

_____

_____

_____

_____

_____

_____

(Total for Question 13 = 3 marks)

14 Explain how to improve anaerobic threshold.

_____

_____

_____

_____

_____

_____

(Total for Question 14 = 3 marks)

15 Analyse how Pilates/yoga or an aerobics class can improve a specific component of fitness.

_____

_____

_____

_____

_____

_____

_____

_____

(Total for Question 15 = 4 marks)

16 What are the long-term effects of training on the body?

_____

_____

_____

_____

_____

(Total for Question 16 = 3 marks)

17 Analyse the effects of EPO.

(a) Advantages:

_____

_____

_____

_____

_____

_____ (2)

(b) Disadvantages:

_____

_____

_____

_____

_____

_____ (2)

(Total for Question 17 = 4 marks)

18 Explain the aims of a warm-up.

_____

_____

_____

_____

_____

_____

(Total for Question 18 = 3 marks)

19 Describe **three** different training methods.

_____

_____

_____

_____

_____

_____

(Total for Question 19 = 3 marks)

20 Complete **Table 5**.

(a) Identify mechanical advantages of first class and second class levers.

(b) Identify mechanical disadvantages of first class and second class levers.

Class of lever	(a) Advantages	(b) Disadvantages
First class	(1)	(1)
Second class	(1)	(1)

Table 5

(Total for Question 20 = 4 marks)

21   Evaluate how various performance-enhancing drugs (PEDs) can affect an athlete.

_____

_____

_____

_____

_____

_____

_____

_____

_____

_____

_____

_____

_____

_____

_____

_____

_____

(Total for Question 21 = 9 marks)

22   Explain the long-term effects of exercise on the muscular, respiratory and cardio-vascular systems.

(a) Muscular system:

_____

_____

_____

_____

_____

_____   (3)

(b) Respiratory system:

_____

_____

_____

_____

_____

_____   (3)

(c) Cardio-vascular system:

_____

_____

_____

_____

_____

_____   (3)

(Total for Question 22 = 9 marks)

TOTAL FOR PAPER = 90 MARKS

Explain the long-term effects of exercise on the muscular, respiratory and other systems.

(a) Muscular System:

Write your name here

Surname		Other names

GCSE

Physical Education

Component 2: Health and Performance

Time: 1 hour and 15 minutes

Paper Reference

1PE0/02

You will need a calculator.

Total Marks

Instructions

- Use **black** ink or ball-point pen.
- Answer **all** questions.
- Answer the questions in the spaces provided.

Information

- The total mark for this paper is 70.
- The marks for **each** question are shown in brackets.
  – use this as a guide as to how much time to spend on each question.

Advice

- Read each question carefully before you start to answer it.
- Check your answers if you have time at the end.

Answer ALL questions.

Write your answers in the spaces provided.

Some questions must be answered with a cross in a box ☒. If you change your mind about an answer, put a line through the box ☒ and then mark your new answer with a cross ☒.

1 (a) Which of the following is the correct definition of progression?

☒	A Training must be coordinated to the requirements of the activity.
☒	B Steadily increase the intensity of activity and keep overloading.
☒	C Gains are only made in fitness when training is more demanding than training previously undertaken.
☒	D Any adaptation will be reversed if you take a break in training.

(1)

(b) Which of the following is the correct definition of overload?

☒	A Training must be coordinated to the requirements of the activity.
☒	B Steadily increase the intensity of activity and keep overloading.
☒	C Gains are only made in fitness when training is more demanding than training previously undertaken.
☒	D Any adaptation will be reversed if you take a break in training.

(1)

(c) Carbohydrates should provide what percentage of an athlete's diet?

☒	A 15%
☒	B 50%
☒	C 60%
☒	D 45%

(1)

(d) A teacher/coach physically manipulating the learner's body is best described as what type of guidance?

☒	A Mechanical
☒	B Manual
☒	C Visual
☒	D Verbal

(1)

(e) Including regular rest/recovery breaks best describes what type of practice?

☒	**A**	Fixed
☒	**B**	Varied
☒	**C**	Massed
☒	**D**	Distributed

(1)

(Total for Question 1 = 5 marks)

2

Overweight and obese men and women, aged 20+, %

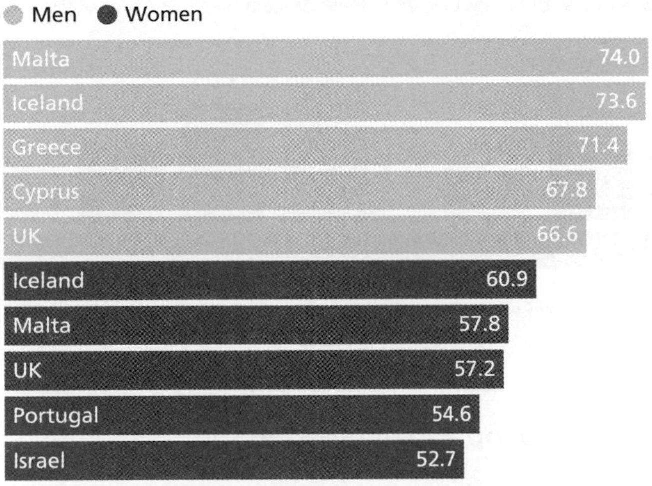

Figure 1

Figure 1 shows obesity rates for males and females in some countries.

Analyse the data in **Figure 1** on obesity levels.

_____

_____

_____

_____

_____

_____

(Total for Question 2 = 3 marks)

3 **How often are people playing sport**

Number of adults taking part in sport at moderate intensity by frequency
■ At least once in last month ■ At least once a week ■ At least twice a week ■ At least three times a week

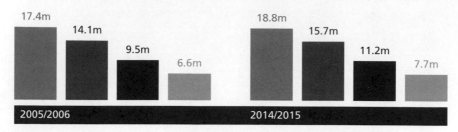

Source: Active People Survey 1 and Active People Survey 9 (Sport England 2005–06 and 2014–15)

Figure 2

Figure 2 shows the number of people taking part in sport in England. Firstly in 2005–2006 and then 2014–2015.

Analyse the data in **Figure 2** to determine the patterns in participation in sport.

_____

_____

_____

_____

_____

_____

(Total for Question 3 = 3 marks)

4   Regular participation in physical activity, such as a spinning class, could reduce the risk of heart disease and stroke.

Identify other risks to long-term health that can be reduced through regular participation in aerobic exercise.

_____

_____

_____

_____

_____

_____

_____

(Total for Question 4 = 3 marks)

5 Describe manual guidance and how it can optimise performance.

....

....

....

....

....

....

....

....

(Total for Question 5 = 3 marks)

6 Explain **two** types of feedback used to optimise performance.

_____

_____

_____

_____

_____

_____

_____

_____

_____

_____

(Total for Question 6 = 4 marks)

7   Evaluate the following types of guidance used to optimise performance.

Mechanical:

_____

_____

_____

_____

_____

_____ (2)

Visual:

_____

_____

_____

_____

_____

_____ (2)

Verbal:

_____

_____

_____

_____

_____

_____ (2)

(Total for Question 7 = 6 marks)

8   Analyse how gender, ethnicity and disability affect participation in sport.

_____

_____

_____

_____

_____

_____

_____

_____

_____

_____

_____

_____

_____

_____

_____ (9)

(Total for Question 8 = 9 marks)

9 Explain the positive health effects of improving fitness.

_____

_____

_____

_____

_____

_____

(Total for Question 9 = 3 marks)

10   Explain reasons why an individual's age could influence their participation in sport.

_____

_____

_____

_____

_____

_____

(Total for Question 10 = 3 marks)

11   Explain commercialism in sport.

_____

_____

_____

_____

_____

_____

(Total for Question 11 = 3 marks)

12   Identify characteristics of emotional health and methods to improve it.

_____

_____

_____

_____

_____

_____

(Total for Question 12 = 3 marks)

13 Explain the following training principles:

Specificity:

_____

_____

Progression:

_____

_____

Overload:

_____

_____

(Total for Question 13 = 3 marks)

14 Explain the importance of macronutrients.

_____

_____

_____

_____

_____

_____

(Total for Question 14 = 3 marks)

15 Explain the importance of micronutrients.

_____

_____

_____

_____

_____

_____

(Total for Question 15 = 3 marks)

16   Explain the classification of simple and complex skills using examples.

Simple:

_____

_____

_____

_____ (2)

Complex:

_____

_____

_____

_____ (2)

(Total for Question 16 = 4 marks)

17 Paul is a 16-year-old GCSE PE student planning a training programme to improve cardio-vascular endurance.

Explain, using examples, how he would use the principles of training.

_____

_____

_____

_____

_____

_____

_____

_____

_____

_____

_____

_____

_____

_____

_____

_____

_____

_____

(Total for Question 17 = 9 marks)

TOTAL FOR PAPER = 70 MARKS

Notes

Answers

Applied Anatomy and Physiology – pages 148–154

Page 148: The Structure and Functions of the Musculo-skeletal System 1

1. Where two parts of the skeleton meet/join/or similar [1]
2. Possible responses: Protection [1]; Movement [1]; Producing red and white blood cells [1]; Producing platelets [1]; Muscle attachment [1]; Storage of calcium and phosphorus [1]. (1 mark for each point made, up to a maximum of 4 marks.)
3. Long bones: Are longer than they are wide [1]; Are hard outside and soft inside [1]; Act as levers [1].
4. Platelets clot the blood [1]; Red blood cells carry oxygen [1]; White blood cells fight disease and infection [1].

Page 149: The Structure and Functions of the Musculo-skeletal System 2

1. Possible responses: Pivot – a bone rotates around another [1]; Hinge – similar to a door and only flexion and extension possible [1]; Ball and socket – are found at the shoulder and the hip and allow movement in three dimensions, or directions [1]; Condyloid – movement is possible in a circular motion [1]. (1 mark for each point made, up to a maximum of 3 marks.)
2. Possible responses: Allows lots of movement [1]; Examples include hip/shoulder [1]; Movement patterns include flexion, extension, adduction, abduction, internal and external rotation [1]; Allows limbs to move in almost every direction [1]. (1 mark for each point made, up to a maximum of 3 marks.)
3. Decreasing angle at a joint [1].

Page 150: The Structure and Functions of the Musculo-skeletal System 3

1. Possible responses: Able to use oxygen [1]; Have lots of capillaries [1]; Red [1]; Contract slowly [1]; Don't fatigue quickly [1]. (1 mark for each point made, up to a maximum of 4 marks.)
2. Possible responses: no oxygen [1]; white [1]; the fastest [1]; powerful [1]; high levels of fatigue [1].

Page 151: The Structure and Functions of the Cardio-respiratory System 1

1. a) Connect veins and arteries [1]
   b) Carry deoxygenated blood to the heart [1]
2. Possible responses: The right atrium receives blood from the body [1]; The blood is forced into the right ventricle [1]; The blood then moves to the lungs [1];

The left atrium receives the blood from the lungs and pushes it to the left ventricle [1]; This blood is then sent around the body [1].
3. a) Blood vessels widen and allow increased blood flow [1]
   b) Blood vessels constrict, getting smaller and tighter, reducing blood flow [1]

Page 152: The Structure and Functions of the Cardio-respiratory System 2

1. Possible responses: Oxygen enters the lungs and bloodstream [1]; Oxygenated blood is pumped to the working muscles [1]; Oxygen is used by the muscles [1]; Carbon dioxide is generated and enters the blood [1]; Deoxygenated blood returns to the heart [1]; From the heart deoxygenated blood then travels to the lungs [1]; Carbon dioxide is removed by the lungs [1]. (1 mark for each point made, up to a maximum of 4 marks.)
2. Possible responses: Breathing gets quicker [1]; Breathing gets deeper [1]; Heart beat and circulation increase [1]; Vasodilation prevents blood pressure getting too high [1]; Vascular shunt mechanism directs the blood to the working muscles [1]; Blood vessels vasodilate (widen) [1]; Blood vessels vasoconstrict (tighten) [1]; Sweat is produced and cools the body [1]. (1 mark for each point made, up to a maximum of 3 marks.)
3. Possible responses: Tiny air sacs with a large surface area where gases are exchanged [1]; Haemoglobin is contained in the red blood cells, and joins oxygen to produce ox-haemoglobin [1]; Red blood cells deliver the oxygen to muscles [1]; Carbon dioxide is removed [1]. (1 mark for each point made, up to a maximum of 3 marks.)

Page 153: Anaerobic and Aerobic Exercise

1. Possible responses: Working at above 80% of MHR [1]; Exercise at high intensity [1]; Interval or fartlek is used to develop [1]; Short duration [1]. (1 mark for each point made, up to a maximum of 3 marks.)
2. Possible responses: The body converts glucose into energy by using oxygen [1]; Every cell in the body requires energy to function [1]; Oxygen is needed at the working muscles to meet demand [1]; Carbon dioxide is breathed out at a greater rate when exercising [1]; Water is lost through sweat, urine or exhalation [1]. (1 mark for each point made, up to a maximum of 4 marks.)
3. Fats [1]; Carbohydrates [1]; Protein [1].

Page 154: The Short- and Long-term Effects of Exercise

1. Rise in muscle temperature [1]; If not enough oxygen is consumed, lactic acid will accumulate and cause pain [1]; If not enough oxygen is consumed, lactic acid will accumulate and fatigue quickly [1].
2. Heart rate increases [1]; Stroke volume increases [1]; Cardiac output increases [1].
3. Possible responses: Help an athlete recover by getting oxygen to the working muscles [1]; Help supply oxygen to the muscles [1]; Help supply oxygen to vital organs [1]; Oxygen is taken into the lungs [1]; Oxygen is transferred to blood [1]; Carbon dioxide is removed [1]. **(1 mark for each point made, up to a maximum of 4 marks.)**

Movement Analysis – pages 155–156
Page 155: Lever Systems

1. The fulcrum is at one end of the lever (sometimes called the **pivot**) and is the point where the load is pivoted [1]; The load is in the middle of the lever, and is the object you are trying to move [1]; The effort is at the opposite end of the lever to the fulcrum, where the force is applied [1].
2. b) [1]
3. Large range of motion [1]; Fast movement is possible [1];The amount of force applied must always exceed the weight of the load [1].

Page 156: Planes and Axes of Movement

1. Sagittal plane is a vertical passing from front to rear separating the body into right and left parts [1]; Frontal plane goes from side to side at right angles to the sagittal plane, it separates the body into a front section and a back section [1]; Transverse plane is a horizontal plane that splits the body into upper and lower parts [1].
2. Frontal axis goes from side to side at right angles to the sagittal plane [1]; Sagittal axis runs horizontally from front to rear lying at right angles to the frontal plane [1]; Vertical axis goes from head to foot at right angles to the transverse plane [1].
3. Possible response/or appropriate other: Rotation in a high board diver somersaulting is an example of movement [1]; In the frontal plane about the sagittal axis [1].

Physical Training – pages 157–165
Page 157: The Relationship between Health and Fitness

1. a) [1]
2. d) [1]
3. Possible responses: Improving physical fitness [1]; Maintaining appropriate body weight [1]; Having a healthy diet [1]; Managing stress [1]; Not smoking [1]; Not drinking alcohol [1]; Not taking drugs [1]. **(1 mark for each point made, up to a maximum of 3 marks.)**

Page 158: Components of Fitness Data Interpretation 1

1. d) [1]
2. a) [1]
3. b) [1]

Page 159: Components of Fitness Data Interpretation 2

1. c) [1]
2. a) [1]

Page 160: The Principles of Training 1

1. Specificity: training needs to be specific to the activity [1]; Progressive: increases in intensity are required [1]; Overload: training must be to a higher intensity than previously for adaptations to occur [1]; Overtraining: if too much training is undertaken, it can result in poor performance, injury and illness [1]; Reversibility: training effects are reversible [1].
2. Can be used to predict if working aerobically [1]; Can be used to predict if working anaerobically [1]; Calculate maximum heart rate by using: 220 – age = MHR [1]; For example, Shelley, aged 20, has maximum heart rate of 220 – 20 = 200 bpm [1]; Heart rate training zone can be calculated using maximum heart rate [1]. **(1 mark for each point made, up to a maximum of 3 marks.)**

Page 161: The Principles of Training 2

1. a) Possible responses: Develops strength [1]; develops cardio-vascular endurance [1]; Targets specific muscle groups [1]; High intensity [1] **(1 mark for each point made, up to a maximum of 3 marks.)**
   b) Possible responses: instructor cannot give individual feedback [1]; Poor technique is not always corrected and can lead to injury [1]
2. Possible responses: Develops flexibility [1]; develops cardio-vascular endurance [1]; good for weight loss [1]; improves coordination [1]; high intensity workout [1]. **(1 mark for each point made, up to a maximum of 4 marks.)**

Page 162: The Long-term Effects of Exercise

1. Possible responses: Train for increased duration [1]; Train at greater intensity [1]; Improved fitness levels [1]; Improved skill levels [1]; Quicker recovery [1]; Improved sleep [1]; Lower resting heart rate [1]; Lower blood pressure [1]; Decreased body fat [1]; Improved health [1]. **(1 mark for each point made, up to a maximum of 4 marks.)**
2. a) Stronger bones [1]
   b) Improved joint stability [1]
   c) Increased size and strength [1]

Page 163: How to Optimise Training and Prevent Injury

1. Used before starting exercise [1]; Recognises potential risks of undertaking physical activity or sport [1]; Participants respond to questions [1]; Identifies a small number of individuals who need to seek further medical advice before exercising [1]; Recommendations can be made to an individual before undertaking exercise [1]; It is still essential to start exercise slowly and increase intensity gradually [1]. **(1 mark for each point made, up to a maximum of 3 marks.)**

2. a) Usually due to direct contact with the head   [1]
   b) One of the bones at a joint is knocked out of place   [1]
   c) Ligaments become stretched at a joint   [1]
   d) Broken or cracked bone or series of bones   [1]
   e) Damage to the surface of the skin   [1]

Page 164: Effective Use of Warm-up and Cool Down

1. Possible responses: Prevent injury [1]; Increased elasticity of ligaments and tendons [1]; Increased range of movement [1]; Increase the temperature of muscles [1]; Increase blood flow [1]; Prepare body for specific exercise [1]. **(1 mark for each point made, up to a maximum of 3 marks.)**

2. Possible responses: Remove lactic acid [1]; Prevent Delayed Onset of Muscle Soreness (DOMS) [1]; Reduce the chance of fainting or dizziness [1]; Maintain and develop flexibility [1]; Reduce muscle temperature [1]; Allow the heart to return to its resting rate [1]. **(1 mark for each point made, up to a maximum of 3 marks.)**

3. a) Pulse raiser   [1]
   b) Dynamic stretching   [1]
   c) Practice activities   [1]
   d) Mental preparation   [1]

Page 165: Use of Data

1. c)   [1]
2. a)   [1]

Health, Fitness and Well-being – pages 166–169

Page 166: Physical, Emotional and Social Health, Fitness and Well-being

1. A state of whole physical, mental and social well-being and with the absence of disease, illness or injury.   [1]
2. The ability to form positive relationships with others and the capability to adjust easily to various social situations and behave fittingly.   [1]
3. a) i)   [1]
   b) iii)   [1]
   c) ii)   [1]

Page 167: The Consequences of a Sedentary Lifestyle 1

1. a) Possible responses, positive impact: Optimal sport performance [1]; Maintain body weight [1]; Improved health [1]. **(1 mark for point made, maximum of 1 mark.)**
   Possible responses, negative impact: Increased risk of chronic heart disease [1]; Diabetes [1]; High blood pressure [1]; Poor physical fitness [1]; Joint pain [1]. **(1 mark for point made, maximum of 1 mark.)**
   b) Possible responses, positive impact: Reduced risk of chronic heart disease [1]; Reduced risk of types of cancer [1]; Lower risk of early death [1]. **(1 mark for point made, maximum of 1 mark.)**
   Possible responses, negative impact: Increased likelihood of gaining body weight [1]; Increased blood pressure [1]; Decreased bone strength [1]; Increased stress [1]; Loss of flexibility [1]; Loss of muscle tone [1]; Loss of fitness [1]; Loss of strength [1]. **(1 mark for point made, maximum of 1 mark.)**

Page 168: The Consequences of a Sedentary Lifestyle 2

1. Possible responses: depression [1]; coronary heart disease [1]; increased blood pressure [1]; types of diabetes [1]; increased risk of osteoporosis [1]; loss of muscle tone [1]; poor posture [1]; poor physical fitness [1]. **(1 mark for each point made, up to a maximum of 5 marks.)**
2. d)   [1]
3. c)   [1]

Page 169: Energy Use, Diet, Nutrition and Hydration

1. a) Possible responses: Quick source of energy [1]; 60% of an athlete's diet [1]; Broken down to glucose [1]. **(1 mark for each point made, up to a maximum of 2 marks.)**
   b) Possible responses: Builds and repairs muscle [1]; Athletes only need 15% in their diet [1]; Athletes consume more protein to aid recovery [1]; Consume after competition and training to recover [1]. **(1 mark for each point made, up to a maximum of 2 marks.)**
2. Vitamins are required to help the body function [1] and aid concentration [1].
3. Possible responses: Sex [1]; Height [1]; Bone structure [1]; Muscle girth [1]. **(1 mark for each point made, up to a maximum of 3 marks.)**

Sport Psychology – pages 170–173

Page 170: Classification of Skills

1. a) Open skill example: a constantly changing environment, e.g. a football pass in a game/accept suitable relevant example [1].
   Closed skill example: a stable environment, e.g. tennis serve/accept suitable relevant example [1].

b) Simple skill example: a straightforward skill that involves little decision-making, e.g. netball pass/ accept suitable relevant example. [1]
Complex skill example: a complicated skill, e.g. gymnastics floor routine/accept suitable relevant example. [1]

2. Possible responses: Continuously repeating a whole skill [1]; Used for closed skills [1]; Continuous form of practice [1]; Used for simple skills [1]; Re-creates game situations as fatigue is caused [1]. **(1 mark for each point made, up to a maximum of 4 marks.)**

Page 171: Goal Setting, SMART Targets and Information Processing

1. Possible responses: Help achieve success [1]; Improvements can be monitored [1]; Show that preparation is effective [1]; Improve confidence [1]; Help motivate the performer [1]; Reduce stress [1]. **(1 mark for each point made, up to a maximum of 3 marks.)**

2. a) Specific: for example, a county footballer could aim to win the cup competition that they are competing in [1].
   b) Measurable: for example, a swimmer trying to achieve a specific time that can be recorded [1].
   c) Achievable: goals need to be set that are realistic and achievable for example a javelin thrower could aim to beat their personal best by 5 metres [1].
   d) Realistic: for example, a junior athlete needs to select goals that are age- and ability-appropriate and realistic [1].
   e) Time-based: a cricket player could aim to achieve a certain amount of wickets by a certain date from matches played [1].

Page 172: Guidance and Feedback on Performance

1. a) Possible responses: Provides mental image, shows what the skill should look like [1]; Supports verbal instruction [1]; Highlight learner error [1]. **(1 mark for point made, maximum of 1 mark.)**
   b) Possible responses: Works well with visual guidance [1]; Good for detailed feedback for advanced performers [1]; Simple coaching points can be used for beginners [1]. **(1 mark for point made, maximum of 1 mark.)**

2. a) Possible responses: Learner can become reliant on the aid [1]; Learner does not get a feel for the skill [1]; Can be demotivating to learner [1]. **(1 mark for each point made, maximum of 1 mark.)**
   b) Participant could be uncomfortable with physical contact [1]; Participant can become reliant on support [1]. **(1 mark for each point made, maximum of 1 mark.)**

3. Intrinsic [1]; Extrinsic [1]; Concurrent [1]; Terminal [1].

Page 173: Mental Preparation, Arousal and Personality

1. Helps to create a positive mindset before competition [1]; Helps to maintain focus [1];

Calms/relaxes the athlete [1]; Helps the athlete to visualise the performance being successful [1].

2. Performer visualising in their mind the correct technique and perfect performance [1].

Socio-cultural Influences – pages 174–178

Page 174: Engagement Patterns of Different Social Groups in Physical Activity and Sport 1

1. Possible responses: Under 50% of females participate in sport [1]; The most popular activity for females is swimming [1]; The second-most popular activity for females is undertaking health and fitness activities and using the gym [1]; Any other relevant point [1]. **(1 mark for each point made, up to a maximum of 3 marks.)**

2. Possible responses: Racism can affect participation in sport and physical activity [1]; There is a lack of specific classes for ethnic minorities [1]; Lack of role models for some ethnic groups [1].

Page 175: Engagement Patterns of Different Social Groups in Physical Activity and Sport 2

1. Possible responses: might not be able to afford equipment required [1]; might not be able to afford to travel to training or games [1]; might not be able to afford to access the facilities [1]; individuals could not be able to afford it as they are unemployed [1]; individuals could not be able to afford it as they are retired [1].

2. Possible responses: might not have enough money [1]; lack of specialist coaches [1]; lack of specialists clubs/ or class [1]; lack of specialist facilities [1]; lack of specialist [1].

Page 176: Commercialisation of Physical Activity and Sport

1. Possible responses: There is a focus on maximising profit at the expense of the values of traditional sport [1]; Brings new audiences to sports [1]; Participation in some sports has increased [1]; Sponsorship has increased income in sport/for performers [1]; Media companies pay huge sums of money for television rights [1]; Media coverage of sport is now extensive [1]. **(1 mark for each point made, up to a maximum of 4 marks.)**

2. a) Increased revenue [1]; Increased support [1].

3. Player/performer tied to wearing specific clothing/ kit [1]; Commercial sponsor appearances can affect performance and training [1].

Page 177: Ethical and Socio-cultural Issues in Physical Activity and Sport

1. Possible responses: Using performance-enhancing drugs [1]; Cheating [1]; Accepting bribes [1]; Fan violence and hooliganism [1]; Illegal betting [1]; Financial irregularities [1]; Player violence [1]; Fielding ineligible players [1]. **(1 mark for each point made, up to a maximum of 4 marks.)**

2. Playing within the rules/being gracious in defeat or victory [1]; Relevant example applied, e.g. shaking an opponent's hand after losing a match [1].

3. Bending the rules/laws of a sport without actually breaking them **[1]**; Relevant example applied, e.g. deliberately missing a free throw **[1]**.

Page 178: Contemporary Sport

1. Possible responses: Frustration of disappointed fans due to the result **[1]**; Poor officiating can cause controversy **[1]**; Provocation by opposing fans or sports performers themselves **[1]**; Religion/tradition **[1]**; Cheating **[1]**; Importance of fixture **[1]**; Any other suitable sporting example **[1]**. **(1 mark for each point, up to a maximum of 3 marks.)**

2. Possible responses: Early kick-offs **[1]**; All-seater stadia **[1]**; Segregation of fans **[1]**; Improved security **[1]**; Alcohol restrictions **[1]**; Travel restrictions/banning orders **[1]**. **(1 mark for each point, up to a maximum of 3 marks.)**

3. a) Possible responses: Increased income/money flows into the sport **[1]**; Role models created to inspire people to take part in sport **[1]**; Encourages participation in the sports covered by TV **[1]**; Amateur participants in sport can learn from television coverage of sports professionals **[1]**; Any other suitable response **[1]**. **(1 mark for each point, up to a maximum of 2 marks.)**

   b) Possible responses: Decreased attendance/people who used to come to matches choose to watch on television instead **[1]**; Only mainstream sports are covered by TV/few sports chosen **[1]**; Change in times of fixtures to suit TV audiences **[1]**; any other suitable response **[1]**. **(1 mark for each point, up to a maximum of 2 marks.)**

Page 179: Use of Data

1. c) **[1]**
2. Face to face **[1]**; Telephone conversations **[1]**; By post **[1]**; Via the internet **[1]**.
3. Bar chart **[1]**; Pie chart **[1]**; Line graph **[1]**.

Page 180 Practice Exam Paper 1

1. (a) A **[1]**
   (b) A **[1]**
   (c) B **[1]**
   (d) D **[1]**
   (e) B **[1]**
   (f) C **[1]**
   (g) A **[1]**
   (h) D **[1]**
   (i) A **[1]**
   (j) C **[1]**

2. Possible responses: For example, in a bicep curl the triceps brachii is the antagonist, the biceps brachii is the agonist **[1]**; Muscles work in antagonistic pairs/pairs of muscles create movement **[1]**; Agonist muscle shortens/is the prime mover **[1]**; Antagonist muscle lengthens/muscle relaxes **[1]**. **(1 mark for correct**

example, e.g. bicep and triceps causing flexion and extension – example must be included to achieve maximum marks – 1 mark for each point made, up to a maximum of 2 marks, for a total of 3 marks.)

3. Possible responses: Ankle plantar-flexion and dorsiflexion creates direction/power **[1]**; Ball and socket joint at the hip allows leg to swing back **[1]**; Hip allows a greater range of movement in the body **[1]**; Hip movement generates more power/direction **[1]**; Accept any other appropriate response **[1]**. **(1 mark for each point made, up to a maximum of 3 marks**

4. Possible responses: Third class lever **[1]**; To move the dumbbell a large amount of effort is required **[1]**; Small movements of the muscles create a long lever movement **[1]**; Fulcrum and load are at different ends of the lever **[1]**; Bicep muscles provide the force and bend the forearm against the weight of the forearm **[1]**; Triceps muscle stabilises the movement/triceps is agonist **[1]**; Effort is off-centre of the lever near the fulcrum/not as effective as a second class lever **[1]**; The pivot is at the elbow and the forearm acts as the lever arm **[1]**. **(1 mark for each point made, up to a maximum of 3 marks.)**

5.

Muscle	(a) Function	(b) Specific sporting movement
Deltoid	Abduction **[1]**	Press-up and bench press/Accept any other appropriate response **[1]**
Hamstring	Flexion **[1]**	Leg curl/Accept any other appropriate response **[1]**

(1 mark for each point, up to a maximum of 4 marks.)

6.

Muscle	(a) Function	(b) Specific sporting movement
Gastrocnemius	Plantar-flexion/point the toes **[1]**	Lunges/Accept any other appropriate response **[1]**
Bicep	Flexion **[1]**	Bicep curls/Accept any other appropriate response **[1]**

(1 mark for each point, up to a maximum of 4 marks.)

7. trachea **[1]**; oxygen **[1]**; heart **[1]**.

8. Possible responses: Protection of vital organs **[1]**; For muscle attachment **[1]**; Joints for movement **[1]**; Production of platelets **[1]**; Red and white blood cell production **[1]**; Storage of calcium and phosphorus

[1]. **(1 mark for each point, up to a maximum of 3 marks.)**

9. Possible responses: Long bones – are longer than they are wide/have a soft centre surrounded by a hard outer casing/are used as levers to enable the body to move/examples include the ulna and tibia, the long leg bones that are used in cycling, running and swimming [1].
   Short bones – are approximately as long as they are wide/have large quantities of bone marrow to make blood vessels/are weight bearing/examples include the carpals and tarsals in the wrist and foot [1].
   Flat bones – are flat and particularly strong/have muscles attached that provide protection/examples include the scapula (shoulder) and the cranium (skull) [1].
   Irregular bones – All remaining bones are classed as irregular bones/they are often unusual in appearance/uses include both protection and muscle attachment/examples include the bones that make up vertebral column (spine) and mandible (jaw) [1].
   (1 mark for each classification of bone explained – only one point needs to be made about each classification to gain 3 marks.)

10. Sagittal plane [1]; Frontal plane [1]; Transverse plane [1].

11. Frontal axis [1]; Sagittal axis [1]; Vertical axis [1].

12. Possible responses: Needs to be at high altitude to be effective [1]; Provides a short-term benefit [1]; There is less oxygen in the air and oxygen-carrying capacity is reduced, therefore the body adapts [1]; The body compensates by making more red blood cells to carry oxygen [1]; Can be beneficial to endurance athletes [1]; Negative effect if altitude sickness occurs [1].
    (1 mark for each point, up to a maximum of 3 marks.)

13. Possible responses: Heart rate needs to be in the aerobic target zone: 60–80% [1]; Exercise at a steady state and not too fast [1]; Examples of methods to improve aerobic threshold, e.g. spinning, aerobics or any other acceptable examples [1]; Oxygen needs to be used/carbon dioxide needs to be removed [1]; Marathon runners use aerobic training or any other acceptable example of activity [1].
    (1 mark for each point, up to a maximum of 3 marks.)

14. Possible responses: Heart rate needs to be in the anaerobic target zone: 80–90% [1]; Anaerobic exercise is needed in short, fast bursts where the heart cannot supply enough oxygen to the muscles [1]; Anaerobic training is needed to improve the ability of the muscles to work without enough oxygen [1]; Working anaerobically will create an oxygen debt/only possible to exercise like this for a short period of time [1]; Oxygen debt is the amount of oxygen consumed during recovery rest [1]; Sprinters use anaerobic training or any other acceptable examples [1]; Examples of methods, e.g. interval training, fartlek training or any other acceptable examples [1]. **(1 mark for each point, up to a maximum of 3 marks.)**

15. Possible responses: Aerobics **(class must be mentioned)** [1]; Exercising to music in a group fitness class/working your body aerobically [1]; Develops strength/flexibility and cardio-vascular endurance [1]; Advantages – Develops flexibility and cardio-vascular endurance/good for weight loss/Improves coordination/high intensity [1]; Disadvantages – can be high impact on the body's joints [1].
    Possible responses: Pilates/yoga **(class must be mentioned)** [1]; Completing a variety of stretches and exercises/Pilates often focuses on the core muscles and all of the body/used for body conditioning [1]; Develops strength and flexibility [1]; Advantages – develops strength and flexibility/targets specific muscle groups [1]; Disadvantages – stretches can be challenging/can lead to injury [1].
    (1 mark for identification of fitness class, 1 mark for an explanation point, 1 mark for an advantage, 1 mark for a disadvantage; to achieve 4 marks – identification, explanation, an advantage and a disadvantage are all required.)

16. Possible responses: Increases ability to train for longer and more intensely [1]; Fitness levels are improved [1]; Motor development in skills is improved [1]; Recovery is quicker [1]; Sleep better [1]; Resting heart rate is lower/bradycardia [1]; Blood pressure is lower [1]; Reduced body fat [1]. Any other suitable response. **(1 mark for each point, up to a maximum of 3 marks.)**

17. (a) Possible responses: Advantages – Increased red blood cell count [1]; Increased oxygen-carrying capacity [1]; Or other relevant advantage [1].
    (b) Disadvantages – Heart problems [1]; Strokes [1]; Or other relevant disadvantage [1]. **(1 mark for each point made, 2 marks maximum for advantages, 2 marks maximum for disadvantages.)**

18. Possible responses: Prevents injury to muscles [1]; Improves elasticity of ligaments/tendons [1]; Increases range of movement [1]; Increases temperature of muscles [1]; Increases blood flow [1]; Prepares the body for specific exercise [1]; Helps an athlete to get into a positive mindset [1]; Helps an athlete to focus [1]; Helps an athlete to relax [1]; Helps an athlete to visualise a performance going well [1]. **(1 mark for each point, up to a maximum of 3 marks.)**

19. Continuous – working at sustained aerobic intensity without rest, for a minimum of 20 minutes. It improves cardio-vascular fitness/endurance [1].

Fartlek – or 'speed play' training incorporates changing your speed, terrain or intensity. It improves speed/aerobic/anaerobic fitness [1].

Circuits – involve performing a series of exercises in a special order, called a circuit. Each activity takes place at a 'station'. It can be designed to improve speed, agility, coordination, balance and muscular endurance [1].

Interval – period of work and relief with varying levels of intensity. It can be used to develop speed and muscular endurance. It improves aerobic and anaerobic fitness [1].

Plyometric – sometimes called jump training. Where muscles are used to exert maximum force in short periods of time, with the aim of developing speed and strength (power). Examples include bounding, jumping and hopping [1].

Weight/resistance – uses weights to provide resistance to the muscles. It can be used to develop muscular strength. By varying weight, sets and reps, different goals can be achieved. Muscular endurance, muscular strength and power can all be developed [1]. **(1 mark for each training method described, up to a maximum of 3 marks.)**

20.

Class of lever	(a) Advantages	(b) Disadvantages
First class	Strong/Stable/Increasing the length of the lever will increase the mechanical advantage. [1]	Slow-acting movement/Limited flexibility [1]
Second class	Strong/Stable/Increasing the length of the lever arm will increase the mechanical advantage. [1]	Slow-acting movement/Limited flexibility [1]

(1 mark for each point, up to a maximum of 4 marks.)

21.

Marks	Comments	Example of answer
2	The level of response is basic and only states the positives of three performance-enhancing drugs. The response does not include any side effects or negatives of using performance-enhancing drugs. There is no conclusion and many performance-enhancing drugs are not included.	Individuals use performance-enhancing drugs in sport to improve their physical performance. There is a big range of substances they can use to improve performance, these include anabolic steroids, which build muscle, increase muscle mass and allow an athlete to train at higher intensity. Another method could be blood doping, which increases the oxygen-carrying capacity of the blood, which in turn means an individual can work at higher intensity with less effort. EPO provides the same benefits to a performer.
5	Like the previous answer, this answer identifies the performance advantages of performance-enhancing drugs, but additionally it includes some potential health risks. It includes a very brief conclusion.	Athletes use performance-enhancing drugs to gain an advantage and to improve their body's cardio-vascular fitness or muscular strength. Some athletes opt to use beta-blockers to help them relax before they compete; additionally it makes the cardio-vascular system work more efficiently. However, it does have some potential negative effects including affecting mental well-being and causing sleep deprivation. Using both EPO and blood doping can increase red blood cell count and increase oxygen-carrying capacity. But both of these effects carry risks of health problems including the risk of heart attack or strokes. Narcotic analgesics can be used to mask pain, but again have severe health risks and are illegal. As you can see there are many advantages and disadvantages of using performance-enhancing drugs.
9	This is an outstanding answer that includes coverage of all the possible performance enhancing drugs. The performance advantages and risks of these drugs are clearly highlighted, and the conclusion rounds off the argument well.	Even though taking performance-enhancing drugs is against the rules of sport and detrimental to an athlete's health, many athletes take the risk as the prospect of winning is so attractive. There are many different performance-enhancing drugs an athlete can use, these include EPO, narcotic analgesics, diuretics, beta blockers, human growth hormones, and anabolic steroids.

		EPO is naturally produced in the body but it can be injected into the body using a synthetic substance to boost the blood's red cell count and oxygen-carrying capacity; this makes significant improvements to aerobic fitness and the body's abilities to recover. EPO does, however, have some severe side effects, including potential heart problems, and the risk of stroke is increased. Withdrawing blood and refrigerating it over several weeks and then injecting it again will have very similar performance benefits, but has the increased risk of infection occurring. Human growth hormones and anabolic steroids both have very similar benefits to an athlete, which include increased muscle mass, which then usually means greater strength and an ability to train harder and recover more quickly. There are, however, significant risks, including heart attack, depression and damage to the kidneys. Diuretics are used to help athletes lose weight, and can also be used to cover up other drugs. Diuretics, like other performance-enhancing drugs, have dangerous side effects, the most notable being the risk of dehydration. Narcotic analgesics are used to allow an athlete to train at a greater intensity and not feel the pain of doing so; these drugs can be very addictive and athletes often struggle to come off them. Beta blockers help reduce levels of stress for performers, causing the cardio-vascular system to work more efficiently. Potential negative effects include disrupted sleep, fatigue and depression. Performance-enhancing drugs have many clear benefits to the body both physiologically and psychologically. However, they are against the rules of sport, not ethical and pose significant health risks.

22. **(a)** Possible responses: Increased bone density – making bones stronger **[1]**; Increased strength of ligaments and tendons – improving joint stability, articular cartilage increases **[1]**; Muscle hypertrophy – muscles become bigger in size, fibres get thicker and stronger **[1]**; The importance of rest for adaptations to take place – without adequate rest changes will not occur **[1]**; It is important to allow adequate time to recover before the next training session **[1]**. **(1 mark for each point, up to a maximum of 3 marks.)**

(b) Possible responses: Increased capillarisation – a greater network of capillaries is created to assist respiration **[1]**; Increase in number of red blood cells, which helps with oxygen transfer to the working muscles **[1]**; Drop in resting blood pressure due to more elastic muscular wall of veins and arteries **[1]**; Increased lung capacity/ volume and vital capacity – means you breathe in more oxygen, the bigger the capacity, the more air comes in **[1]**; Increased number of alveoli – results in more efficient gaseous exchange **[1]**;

Increased strength of diaphragm and external intercostal muscles – results in greater force and less likelihood of fatigue **[1]**. **(1 mark for each point, up to a maximum of 3 marks.)**

(c) Possible responses: Decreased resting heart rate – as your heart becomes stronger and more efficient more blood is pumped per beat, so resting heart rate is reduced **[1]**; Faster recovery – after long-term training athletes are able to recover more quickly **[1]**; Increased resting stroke volume – more blood is pumped per heart beat **[1]**; Increased maximum cardiac output – more blood is pumped per minute **[1]**; Increased size/strength of heart – the heart becomes bigger and stronger **[1]**. **(1 mark for each point, up to a maximum of 3 marks.)**

Page 200 Practice Exam Paper 2

1. **(a)** B   [1]
   (b) C   [1]
   (c) C   [1]
   (d) B   [1]
   (e) D   [1]

2. Possible responses: Obesity for males is highest in Malta [1]; Obesity for females is highest in Iceland [1]; From Figure 1 males have the lowest obesity rates in the United Kingdom [1]; From Figure 1 females have the lowest obesity rates in Israel [1]; Or other relevant point [1]. **(1 mark for each point, up to a maximum of 3 marks.)**

3. Possible responses: The amount of people participating in sport at least once a month has increased [1]; The amount of people participating in sport at least once a week has increased [1]; The amount of people participating in sport at least twice a week has increased [1]; The amount of people participating in sport at least three times a week has increased [1];The biggest rise in participation has been twice a week [1]; The lowest rise in participation has been three times a week [1]; Or other relevant point [1]. **(1 mark for each point, up to a maximum of 3 marks.)**

4. Possible responses: Depression [1]; Coronary heart disease [1]; High blood pressure [1]; Diabetes [1]; Increased risk of osteoporosis [1]; Loss of muscle tone [1]; Poor posture [1]; Poor physical fitness [1]. **(1 mark for each point, up to a maximum of 3 marks.)**

5. Possible responses: Teacher/coach physically manipulating the learner's body [1]; Through the correct movement pattern [1]; Teacher/coach supporting a learner, e.g. learning a handstand [1]. **(Any other suitable responses accepted.)**

6. Intrinsic feedback – Tells the performer if the skill felt right [1]; It can be self-motivating [1]. Extrinsic feedback – Feedback given by teacher/coach/fans [1]; Rewarding to the individual [1]. Concurrent feedback – Information provided to the athlete during the performance [1]; Can be used to alter performance whilst active [1]. Terminal feedback – Information provided to the athlete before or after the performance [1]; Can help the athlete evaluate overall performance [1]. **(1 mark for each type of feedback, up to 2 marks, 1 mark for each explanation, up to 2 marks, a total of 4 marks available.)**

7. Possible responses: Mechanical – Helps to build confidence, good for dangerous skills, breaks the skill down to make teaching easier (advantage) [1]; Learner can become reliant on the aid/learner does not get a feel for the skill/can be demotivating to learner (disadvantage) [1].
Visual – Provides mental image, shows what the skill should look like/supports verbal instruction/highlights learner error (advantage) [1]; Learner can lose motivation if the skill is too difficult/needs to be accurate demonstration otherwise learning will not take place/can't copy movement (disadvantage) [1].
Verbal – Learner can lose motivation if the skill is too difficult/needs to be accurate demonstration otherwise learning will not take place/can't copy movement (advantage) [1]; Amount of information needs to be limited for beginners, does not work well for complex skills/can be boring (disadvantage) [1].
(1 mark maximum given for one advantage of each type of guidance, 1 mark maximum given for one disadvantage of each type of guidance.)

8.

Marks	Comments	Example of answer
2	The level of response is undeveloped and only identifies participation patterns. The response fails to develop any reasons why an individual's participation could be affected. There is no conclusion or evaluation. The response also displays limited elements of knowledge and understanding, with little use of technical language.	Statistically women participate less in sport than men and there are many reasons for this. If people do not have a significant disposable income they cannot afford to participate in sport. Like women, ethnic minorities often have low participation, this can be partly because of racism. The final group that I'm going to talk about is people with disabilities. They often also have low participation as it can be tricky to participate.
6	This covers the required content well and displays some good understanding. Knowledge is applied to the question but the answer would not score higher as it fails to come to an appropriate conclusion.	There are fewer opportunities for women in sport, for example there is a lack of sufficient women-only sessions in gyms and leisure centres. Also some women fear being judged or lack the confidence to take part in sport and physical activity. The opportunities for women in sport are slowly increasing but they are still low in some areas. Some religious values do not promote women taking part in sport. Ethnicity and racist behaviour can prevent individuals from taking part in sport, again, like women, the lack of sufficient specific classes can be a problem. Lack of roles models for people to aspire to can also be an issue. The participation of ethnic minorities in sport is increasing. The number of disabled people who take part in

		sport has risen significantly but barriers remain, for example funding can be an issue as well as a lack of specialist coaches, clubs, classes and facilities.
9	This is an excellent answer and includes coverage of all the required areas. The answer displays the correct knowledge and understanding, and uses technical language. Knowledge is applied to the question throughout and an excellent conclusion is made.	Physical activity and participation in sport can be affected by many factors. There are many groups of people who have lower participation, these include disabled people, young people, old people, ethnic minorities, women and also individuals with less disposable income. In the United Kingdom ethnic minorities often have low rates of participation in sport, however participation is slowly increasing. There are many factors that can affect participation in sport by individuals from an ethnic minority. Racist behaviour can prevent individuals from taking part in sport, and a lack of sufficient specific classes is often an issue. Additionally, for some ethnic minorities there are not many role models for people to aspire to. Religious beliefs can affect participation for some ethnic minorities. There are fewer opportunities for women to undertake sport and physical activity, for example there is a lack of sufficient women-only sessions in gyms and leisure centres. Some religious values do not promote the participation of women in sport. School physical education is often male-oriented and does not provide enough opportunities for girls to participate, and this gender bias and poor changing facilities can adversely affect motivation in wanting to participate. Some women fear being judged or lack the self-esteem to take part in sport. The opportunities for women in sport are slowly increasing, but are still low in some areas. For disabled participants sport and physical activity can be extremely challenging. For example, having specialist coaching, equipment and facilities can be problematic for participants and being able to access appropriate transport can be challenging. Often individuals with disabilities need individual tailored support. The number of disabled people who take part in sport has risen significantly but barriers remain, for example funding can be an issue.

9. Possible responses: Help prevent cardiovascular disease [1]; Help prevent diabetes [1]; Prevent certain types of cancer [1]; Reduce blood pressure [1]; Reduce obesity [1]; Reduce depression [1]; Reduce osteoporosis [1]; Improve social skills [1]. (1 mark for each point, up to a maximum of 3 marks.)

10. Possible responses: Physically demanding sports are usually chosen by younger people, for example rugby, football, netball, hockey [1]; People who are older most often participate in sports that have less demanding strenuous impact, for example swimming and walking [1]; Younger people often cite lack of time for participation in sport [1]; Older people often cite ill health as a reason not to participate in sport [1]; Lack of age-specific groups/clubs can affect participation [1]; The introduction of veterans' walking football has helped increase participation [1]; Some older people can have lots of free time for physical activity or sport [1]; Some young people can have lots of free time for physical activity or sport [1]. (1 mark for each point, up to a maximum of 3 marks.)

11. Possible responses: Commercialism is the emphasis on making money out of sport [1]; Commercialism and sport are closely linked in the twenty-first century [1]; Possibility that commercialism maximises profit at the expense of the values of a sport [1]; Commercialism brings new audiences to sports and can increase participation in some sports [1]; Sponsorship has increased income for sports/individual performers [1]; Media companies pay huge sums of money for television rights to some sports [1]; Most clubs have sponsors/most competitions/stadia now have sponsors [1]. (1 mark for each point, up to a maximum of 3 marks.)

12. Possible responses: Characteristics – Able to control emotions [1]; In control of behaviour [1]; Able to

adapt to change and deal with challenges [1]; Have positive relationships [1]; Able to bounce back from negative experiences [1]. Improved through – Undertaking physical activity [1]; Getting enough rest and sleep [1]; Good nutrition [1]; Limiting alcohol and avoiding cigarettes [1]; Managing individual stress levels [1]. **(1 mark for each point, up to a maximum of 3 marks.)**

13. Possible responses: Specificity: training must match the requirements of the activity/sport/individual fitness levels [1]; Progression: increasing the intensity of training, doing this too quickly can lead to illness, injury or overtraining [1]; Overload: adaptations occur when you work harder than before/overload occurs through increasing the level of either frequency/ intensity/duration (time)/type of training. [1] **(1 mark for each point, up to a maximum of 3 marks.)**

14. Possible responses: Carbohydrates – Provide quick energy [1]; Break down to glucose to provide fast-release energy [1]; Athletes consume carbohydrates (carb-load) in preparation for a sporting event [1]. Protein – Builds and repairs muscle [1]; Athletes consume more protein to aid recovery after competition and training [1]; Power athletes, e.g. a high-jumper, require protein [1]. Water – Helps to maintain levels of hydration/prevents dehydration [1]; It is important not to drink too much water or hypernatremia can be caused, which can be fatal as levels of salt and sodium can become dangerously low [1]. Fibre – Is indigestible and helps to prevent constipation [1]; Aids healthy digestion [1]; Helps to maintain body weight [1]. **(1 mark for each point, up to a maximum of 3 marks – name of macronutrient must be included.)**

15. Possible responses: Minerals help to break down energy from food [1]; Are required to help intensive training and competition [1]; Calcium strengthens bones [1]; Iodine is needed for energy production [1]; Iron prevents fatigue [1]. Vitamins are required to help the body function [1] and aid concentration [1]. Fats – Unsaturated fats are beneficial to health [1]; Are a source of slow-release energy [1]; Are a source of energy for aerobic exercise [1]. **(1 mark for each point, up to a maximum of 3 marks – name of micronutrient must be included.)**

16. Possible responses, simple: Straightforward [1]; Little attention is required [1]; Not many sub-routines [1]; Very few decisions to be made [1]; Pass in football/or other suitable example [1].
Possible responses, complex: clear focus and devotion is needed [1]; Difficult [1]; Performed in preparation frequently [1]; Lots of sub-routines [1]; Tennis serve/or other suitable example [1]. **(1 mark for explanation of each skill, 1 mark for an example of each skill, up to 2 marks, a total of 4 marks available.)**

17.

Marks	Comments	Example of answer
3	The level of response is rudimentary and shows limited knowledge, evaluation and conclusion. The response does correctly identify specificity, and that to overload is required to develop the body. The response does correctly identify that working in the aerobic zone is necessary and cycling is given as an example. Rest is also highlighted as important. To achieve higher marks more examples are needed, greater explanation should be included and a developed conclusion added.	When trying to improve cardio-vascular endurance you need to make sure that your training is the same fitness component and specific to what you are aiming to do. In this instance you will need to do continuous training and will need to work in the aerobic zone. Also to improve you will need to gradually overload your body and increase weekly to have progression. Also it is important to allow for rest when doing continuous training, for example cycling would be a good idea.
5	Similar to the previous answer, this answer identifies the principles of training, which are specificity, progression, overload, rest, reversibility and tedium. Knowledge is applied to the question about improving cardio-vascular endurance, however the summary and evaluation are limited. Some brief examples are given, and more detailed explanations are required.	To improve cardio-vascular endurance you need to use the principles of training. They are specificity, progression, overload, rest, reversibility and tedium. Firstly you need to make sure that your training methods are specific to the individual's needs, for example undertaking a continuous method working in the aerobic zone. This could be achieved by running at 70%–80% of maximum heart rate. Also, you need to gradually improve your training and overload. If you don't train reversibility will occur and you will lose training gain, this happens three times faster on average than your training advances. Deterioration

		sets in after about one week. Also it is important to have variety in your training to prevent tedium and boredom. To sum up, it is important to use all the principles of training – specificity, progression, overload, rest, reversibility and tedium.
9	This is an excellent answer that includes all the required information and gives detailed explanations with examples for specificity, progression, overload, rest, reversibility and tedium. Knowledge is applied to the question with a range of examples, such as using running as a method to improve cardio-vascular endurance training and varying this training with interval, fartlek or continuous training. Another example provided is the use of free weights as a way of improving muscular strength. A conclusion is included and advantages and disadvantages of the system are highlighted.	To improve cardio-vascular endurance the principles of training need to be used, and the principles are: specificity, progression, overload, rest, reversibility and tedium. Specificity means that training needs to be specific to improving cardio-vascular endurance, therefore in this instance the training needs to be continuous training or possibly interval training. The same muscle groups that are used need to be targeted and maximum heart rate should be at 70%–80%. An example could be a marathon runner doing mostly endurance training. The training programme should include progression with gradual increases in demand that would allow the body to progressively adapt to the training demands placed on it, as it gradually gets fitter. By gradually increasing intensity, overload occurs. It is essential that this does not occur too quickly as injury or illness can occur if this happens. An example is someone trying to improve their cardio-vascular endurance for swimming; each week they could add a couple of lengths on to their swimming session or they could try and do the same sessions a bit quicker. All training is reversible and if no training occurs training gains will be lost. This usually happens three times quicker than gains are made and deterioration sets in after about one week – muscles that are not used waste away or atrophy occurs where they become smaller. It is also important that if someone is trying to improve their cardio-vascular endurance they allow time to rest and recover so that adaptations can occur. Finally, having variety in the training is vital to maintain motivation and prevent tedium. For example, if someone uses running as a method of improving cardio-vascular endurance training, they could vary it by doing interval, fartlek or continuous training. To conclude, it is really important that the principles of training are applied in order to achieve maximum performance gains. It is also important that the correct training method is carefully chosen so that it matches the physical attributes that are being improved. For example, using free weights is a good method of improving muscular strength.

Notes

Notes